UNEMPLOYMENT

The Shocking Truth of Its Causes,
Its Outrageous Consequences
And What Can Be Done About It

by **Jack Stone**
and Joe McCraw

This book is dedicated to Jack's daughter, Meechal and son, Yuval, to his sister Maisie who provided the indispensable encouragement without which this book could never have been written and to all working people adversely affected one way or another by the outrageous institution of mass unemployment.

Dear Reader To contact Jack Stone, please call my home phone 415-472-2976 or e-mail to jakstone1@comcast.net

Acknowledgements

Joe McCraw is a political activist. He graduated with a BA in Anthropology from UCSC in 2004. He then moved to Rio de Janeiro to learn Portuguese and study land reform movements (M.S.T.). Joe is the administrator of MediatedThought.com a social activism website. He currently resides on Treasure Island in the San Francisco Bay.

A person who deserves special thanks is my assistant, Virginia Kalagorgevitch, who stood by me all the eight years it took me to do this book.

I must also express my gratitude to Congressman John Conyers and his staff for their help in providing the information on the full employment law proposals of the 1980s and the 1990s.

I also owe a special debt of gratitude to Carol Nelson, Kathrina and Mica Nopuente, Danica Obligacion, Brian Buckley and Ken Dickinson.

Others who have very kindly given me of their time and their advice were Jamie Ginsberg, Harold Abend, Sue Ellen Raby, Henry Schreibman, Luciana Brito, Doreen Stock, Michael Harr, Irene Favreau, Bette-Lou Woods, Hazel Jaramillo, Arthur George, Steve Henneman, and Winnie Pablo.

Special thanks are also owed to Elmer Jan, Tom McGibney, Damon Hill, Livia Lewin, Carol Uhrmacher, and Laurie Thompson, all of the reference desk of the Marin County Civic Center Library in San Rafael, California.

Sincere thanks goes to Michael Rosenthal of San Rafael, California, for his copyediting and proofreading.

My deepest thanks goes to the following publishers who have granted permission to quote passages or to reproduce graphic materials from their books:

The Free Press, a Division of Simon & Schuster Adult Publishing Group for passages from *History of American Labor* by Joseph G. Rayback.

Simon and Schuster for *The Secret Diary of Harold L. Ickes, Vol. II: The Inside Struggle, 1936-1939* by Harold L. Ickes.

The New Press for *From the Folks Who Brought You the Weekend: A Short Illustrated History of Labor in the United States* by Priscilla Murolo and A.B. Chitty.

The American Prospect for Lester Thurow, "*The Crusade That's Killing Prosperity*," and Robert Reich "*It's the Year 2000 Economy, Stupid*".

Multinational Monitor for *Sewing Discontent in Nicaragua* by Leia Raphaelidas and *Aiding and Abetting Corporate Flight: U.S. Aid in the Caribbean Basin* by Barbara Briggs.

Monthly Review Press for *A History of Capitalism 1500-1980* by Michael Beaud.

The New York Review of Books for The New Ruthless Economy by Simon Head.

UE Press for *Labor's Untold Story* by Richard O. Boyer and Herbert M. Morais.

South End Press for *Strike!* by Jeremy Brecher,

William Greider for *One World Ready or Not* and *Secrets of the Temple*

The New York Times for *A 20-year G.M. Parts Migration* by Sam Dillon.

Houghton Mifflin for *The Coming of The New Deal* by Arthur Schlesinger, Jr.

CARTOONS

The first and most deeply felt acknowledgement I must make is to Peter Gilmore of the United Electrical, Radio and Machine Workers of America (UE) for granting me permission to use the many brilliant cartoons by Fred Wright. Peter has been not only kind but has provided much encouragement.

I am no less grateful to Gary Huck and Mike Konopacki for their several wonderful cartoons and to Jeff Danziger for his hilarious cartoon on the export of jobs to China.

I must also express my gratitude to Jan Bunch of Tribune Media Services for her kind response to my request to use Jeff MacNelly's cartoon on the issue of underemployment.

Cartoons by Fred Wright: pp. 41, 96, 99, 102, 104, 105, 112, 115, 127, 206, 217

Cartoons by Gary Huck and Mike Konopacki: pp. 88, 204

Cartoon by Danziger: p. 126

Cartoon by Jeff MacNelly p. 21

Contents

Preface

I have decided to write this book because the issue of unemployment is shrouded in half-truths and outright lies. As a result, there is almost total ignorance about the real causes of unemployment and worse still, about its very serious consequences. Many claim that there are enough jobs but that the unemployed are lazy and would rather be on welfare. While this may be true of a very small fraction of the unemployed, it is not true of the overwhelming majority. There have been numerous instances in which whenever advertisements calling for applicants for relatively well-paid jobs or for jobs that paid better than the minimum wage, the number of applicants that applied for those jobs were ten or more times greater than the number of jobs that were advertised.

On September 26th of 1984, to mention just one instance, the Associated Press News Agency reported that "50,000 people lined up for 350 jobs." The report went on to say that "the applicants, some of whom waited in line for two days, hope to land a longshoreman's job paying $15.45 an hour or a marine clerk's job earning $17.45 an hour... However the fact that only 350 jobs are currently available didn't dismay the crowd, which queued up in a line in the San Pedro district [of Los Angeles] that stretched for 13 miles..."

Clearly, the majority would rather have gainful employment at a living wage and live a life of dignity and integrity. Furthermore, apart from the simple need to earn a living, productive employment is an indispensable part of the psychological makeup of human beings. Simply put, people want to feel useful. Prolonged joblessness is a serious threat to a person's self-esteem and destroying that self-esteem has appalling consequences.

The ugly truth is that the system under which we live will not or cannot provide jobs for those who need them. The business class is simply not interested in full employment because mass unemployment provides them with many benefits. Among those benefits: a large pool of unemployed workers drives down the wages employers have to pay.

The animus of this book is not directed at all business owners. Many if not most owners of businesses would be horrified to learn that the representatives of major business organizations and their allies in Congress have acted against and succeeded in defeating all attempts to enact laws that would create full or near full employment. We also have no doubt that many business people would not use mass unemployment to take advantage of their employees. We are also aware that many business owners work very hard, are kind to their employees, and have great difficulty in keeping their businesses alive. The major business organizations have been against full employment because it brings them many benefits as will be seen in chapter six. Like any other institutions presently part of the structure of America's capitalist economy, mass unemployment is one of the more important pillars that holds up that structure. The business class has therefore held on to it with great tenacity as will be seen in chapters three and five.

In the chapters that follow, we have used a number of concepts to include what we mean by the owners of business. They are: employers, business people, business class, the corporations, the corporate investor class. Whatever differences readers may find among those concepts, our purpose is to show that it is the owners of businesses, whether small, medium or large, that gain from mass unemployment. Some of them gain little or very little and some gain much or very much, but nearly all gain to some extent.

Mass unemployment and under-employment affects not only the jobless and the partially jobless; it also has profoundly negative consequences for every person living in the U.S. What if every person who needed a job had one that paid a decent and living wage and was treated with respect? Would there be as much crime as there is at present? Would there be as much conflict within families as we have at present? Would there be as many divorces? Would there be as much spouse and child abuse and family murders? Would there be as many robberies, muggings, break-ins, assaults and murders? Would homeowners and apartment owners need to fence their properties and shutter their windows? Would we need an army of security guards? Would we need to spend as many hundreds of billions of dollars as we do at present in maintaining a law enforcement system to protect our homes and ourselves?

If every person who needed a job had one and was paid well enough to support a life of dignity, we would not need as many prisons and the billions of dollars to maintain them. Nor would we need to spend hundreds of billions of dollars to protect our cars, our homes, our personal property and ourselves by installing expensive security devices. Also many billions of tax dollars now spent on welfare and unemployment compensation could be spent on creating badly needed jobs. All Americans would also benefit from the billions of dollars in tax revenues that would be paid by the millions of the currently unemployed. These taxes could go into the federal treasury thus reducing our own individual tax burden. Nor would we have had to forgo the trillions of dollars worth of goods and services that would have been produced over the last hundred and more years if all the millions of the unemployed had steady jobs.

This book has been written mainly for working people in all their diversity whose main income derives from working for

others, for the many millions of American workers who find
themselves unemployed, for those who are threatened with unemployment, and for those who spend most if not all of their
lives without jobs. Above all, it has been written for all those
people concerned about the social health and well-being of the
country in which we all live.

This book does not take a neutral stand on the issue of mass
unemployment. How else can one relate to this issue when one
becomes aware of the cruel fact that unemployment is deliberately created? It is an effort to expose capitalism's most outrageous feature – its compulsive need to use unemployment and
the fear of unemployment to ensure the docility and subservi-
ence of its workers. Under the capitalist system, the stick of the
fear of unemployment is necessary to keep workers' noses to
the grindstone and make them perform to the satisfaction of
their employers. The stick is needed because much work is bor-
ing, the carrot paid is less than a living wage, provides workers
very little or no control over the work process, and stifles creativity. Under a different system, one in which working people
participated fully in the decisions affecting what, how and for
what purpose goods and services were produced; if we had a
system based on economic democracy, there would be no need
to use the stick of the fear of unemployment. The creativity of
most of the millions of working people, now mostly dormant,
would be awakened and the volume and quality of improvements and inventions especially in housing, energy, transit systems and health care would be so great as to tower high above
and completely overshadow the number and purpose of the
innovations created under the present system.

Introduction

How the Public Is Deceived About the Issue of Unemployment and About Related Matters of Concern to Working People

On November 7, 2003, W. Michael Cox, chief economist of the Federal Reserve Bank of Dallas coauthored an op-ed article in the New York Times entitled "The Great Job Machine."

"Large-scale upheaval in jobs is part of the economy;" he wrote, "the impetus for it comes from technology, changing trade patterns and shifting consumer demand. History tells us that the result will be ever more jobs, greater productivity and higher incomes for American workers in general.

"New Bureau of Labor Statistics data covering the past decade show that job losses seem as common as sport utility vehicles on the highways. Annual job loss ranged from a low of 27 million in 1993 to a high of 35.4 million in 2001. Even in the year 2000 when the unemployment rate hit its lowest point of the 1990's expansion, 33 million jobs were eliminated." And then, "according to the Labor Bureau's figures, annual job gains ranged from 29.6 million in 1993 to 35.6 million in 1999."

The article is wonderful in the number of important facts it omits. For instance, Cox is dead silent on how many of the annual job gains were part-time, insecure and mind numbing and on how many of those jobs, both full– and part-time, paid less than a living wage with few or no benefits. Nor does he tell us that many part-time workers have been compelled to work two or three jobs to make ends meet. Mr. Cox also very convenient-

5

ly says nothing about the millions of discouraged workers who have stopped looking for work and are therefore not included in the unemployment count of the Labor Department's Bureau of Statistics.

"Day in and day out," Cox writes, "workers quit their jobs or get fired, then move on to new positions. Companies start up, fail, downsize, upsize, and fill the vacancies of those who left. It is workers migrating to new and existing jobs that keeps the country from sinking into some depression-like swamp."

"....fill the vacancies of those who left," Cox writes. Had he been living in the real world, he would have said that many of the jobs left vacant were well-paid jobs and are filled not by workers but by thousands of computers, robots and other advanced technologies introduced by corporations or sent abroad to India, Pakistan and elsewhere where wages are a fraction of what was paid to American workers. And the purpose of all this displacement of American workers is driven by an insatiable hunger for profits.

And then comes Cox's classical understatement of the woes that jobless workers have to face. "Yes, this disruption can be very hard on some workers who lose their employment and have trouble adapting."

Let's pause, a minute, Mr. Cox. You glossed over a very severe issue. "Very hard" needs to be spelled out. If you would have taken the trouble to go and have an intimate look into the lives of the unemployed, you would see a world in which many of them suffer horrendous consequences. Not having a job or losing hope of ever finding one or being jobless for a prolonged period can mean the proverbial last straw on the camel's back. It can mean that many jobless working people already saddled with other problems – family, financial or otherwise – can sink into a state of chronic depression which, in too many cases, leads to the abuse of alcohol, to drugs, to spousal or child abuse and to the breakup of families. And yes, in some of the worst cases, even to suicides and homicides.

"But in a larger sense," he writes, "the turmoil of the labor market is vital to economic progress." Economic progress for whom, he doesn't say. Millions of well-paid jobs have been eliminated, either by the ceaseless introduction of new technology or by their export to other countries where working people are paid a fraction of what is paid in the United States. This vast loss of well paid and mostly unionized jobs has forced millions of American workers – those who are still working – into jobs whose average wages have plummeted at least twenty percent since the 1970s. But he is right if what he meant by economic progress has been the excellent economic progress both in wealth and income made by the top ranks of the corporate-investor class.

A fact of utmost importance that Michael Cox failed to mention is that without the enormous economic stimulation provided by all levels of government in this country, there would have been a total downfall of the system instead of the "economic progress" that he mentions.

Most people, if they even pause to think about it, believe that it is the so-called "free enterprise" capitalist system that creates the jobs needed by millions of the country's working people. That is only partly true. But few, if any, are aware that many millions of jobs are created directly and indirectly by all levels of government: federal, state, counties, and cities. When spent, the many billions of dollars that those government jobs generate provide the profit margins needed to prop up what would otherwise be a wobbly system. In the year 2001, for instance, all levels of government employed 20,970,000 employees full and part time and they were paid $60,632,000,000. These did not include employees of the Central Intelligence Agency, the National Security Agency, the Defense Intelligence Agency, and the National Imagery and Mapping Agency.[1]

But it is not only those vast networks of government jobs that sustain the system. In 2002, the Federal government created many jobs – several hundred thousand jobs is a reasonable estimate – by granting prime contracts worth $180,600,000,000 most of which were given to corporations that produce aircraft, electronics, communication equipment, missiles and space systems, ships, tanks, ammunition and weapons for the military. In 2003, it granted $219,500,000,000 for the same purpose.[2]

Furthermore, the Department of Homeland Security spent a total of $42,447,200,000 in 2003, $41,307,100,000 in 2004, and a requested $47,385,700,000 for 2005. It's impossible to say how many jobs were thus created but could it have been an insignificant number?[3]

In 2002, the federal government also provided $1,368,300,000,000, [that is $1 trillion, 368 billion and 300 million] in the form of credits.[4] In fact, in 2003 the federal government alone spent a total of $2,140,400,000,000 – that is 2 trillion, 140 billion and 400 million dollars.[5] What is that if not a giant prop for the system? Yet another prop, holding up an otherwise chronically unstable system, are the billions of dollars worth of tax cuts doled out mainly to the very rich. And when these tax cuts are granted, it is always justified by declaring that corporations will invest those cuts in creating needed jobs. How many jobs such tax cuts create is difficult to know for there is no government agency tracking the use of those cuts. If the market is already saturated with goods and services, what incentive is there for corporations to invest in creating jobs? In fact, businesses have been known to use their tax cuts for purposes other than creating jobs. During the Reagan administration, for instance, many corporations used their millions of dollars in cuts to acquire other corporations.[6]

It is important to note that the millions of jobs created by all levels of government are generally the ones that are more likely to be secure and pay relatively decent wages and salaries, and therefore have ripple effects. Persons with good income buy more goods and services than others, thus creating jobs for a host of service industries such as bank, insurance companies, retail and wholesale outlets, restaurants, hotels, etc.,

In sum, therefore, governments at all levels create the millions of jobs without which the capitalist system would have great difficulty sustaining itself. It is interesting to note that while governments create the very jobs that sustain the so-called free enterprise system, the advocates of that system never cease to vilify government by demanding that 'it get off our backs.'

One of the many wonders of our politics is that when our Presidents brag about the many millions of jobs their Administrations create, they are dead silent about the fact that many of those jobs are part time, poorly paid and insecure. Many of the workers employed in these low-income jobs are compelled to work two or three jobs to make ends meet.

According to official statistics, in the year 2003, for instance, there were 7,315,000 part time workers. Most of the part-time workers were whites 25-54 years old, and they comprised 6,273,000 of the total.[7] But these figures do not include a vast array of part-time work paid for under the table.

But that is not the end of the story. Commenting on the role of the federal government in sustaining the [capitalist] economy,

Lewis Lapham, the editor of Harper's magazine writes: "For ten years I have listened to self-styled entrepreneurs (men of vision, men of genius, etc.) bang their fists on grillroom tables and complain of the thousand and one ways in which government regulations strangled their initiative and bound the arm of honest labor. I'm sure that much of what they said was true, but never once did I hear any of them acknowledge their abject dependence on the gifts of government subsidy – the mortgage deductions on residential real estate, myriad investment credits and tax exemptions, preferential interest rates, Social Security payments, subsidies to entire industries (defense, real estate, agriculture, highway construction, etc.), tariffs, the bankruptcy laws, the licenses granted to television stations, the banking laws, the concessions given to the savings and loan associations."[8]

The most glaring aspect of Cox's deception was his total omission of the Taft-Hartley Act, one of the severest blows dealt to working people in America's history. That Act, enacted in 1947 by a Congress dominated by the allies of business, has since the 1980s been responsible for the gradual erosion of the living standards of many working people.

To understand why the anti-worker Taft-Hartley Act was enacted, one must go back to the 1935 Wagner Act. The Wagner Act stated "Nothing in this Act…shall be construed so as to either interfere with or impede or diminish in any way the right to strike, or to affect the limitations or qualifications on that right." Thus, in essence, the Wagner Act provided workers the much needed freedom to organize in order to withstand the overwhelming power of their employers.

That freedom was robbed by the Taft Hartley Act which also made it very difficult for workers to use the strike – their only effective weapon in their struggle for maintaining or improving their working conditions.

"Taft-Hartley made it possible for employers who campaign aggressively against unions to disseminate anti-union messages even if they are false. Employers can hold mandatory captive audience meetings in the workplace but unions have no right to respond in the workplace. Union organizers who are not employees have no right to be on the employer's property, but an employer is free to hire a union-busting consultant and have its staff on the premises every day. Supervisors have no legal protection if they refuse to participate in the employer's anti-union campaign. Many employers engage in illegal practices, such as firing or otherwise discriminating against union supporters because they know that the penalties for doing so are pitifully small. In collective bargaining, the penalty for an employer bargaining in bad faith is usually simply an order from the National Labor Relations Board to return to the bargaining table. An employer suffers no monetary penalty for bad faith bargaining, so is it any wonder that employers routinely refuse to reach agreement with unions representing their employees? If the workers strike, it is legal for the employer to hire permanent replacements, and many companies have done so."[9]

One example of how Taft-Hartley had adversely affected workers occurred in 1994 at the Overnite Transportation Company. "In 1994, when the 14,000 workers at Overnite began an organizing drive to join the Teamsters Union, they were faced in the words of Jim Douglas, Overnite's president with 'fury of the Overnite machine.'"

Bargaining between the two sides dragged on for seven years and even though the conflict was settled in favor of the union, Overnite appealed the verdict. It was only in 2002, eight years after the union drive began, that the Courts made a decision that justified the claims of the union but still left the workers without a union. For as Overnite deliberately dragged the negotiations on for eight years, many workers became discouraged and many eventually returned to work. The Teamsters finally called an end to the strike.[10]

In 1991, one labor leader told of what workers and their unions had to go through when trying to organize themselves into a union.

"…It's more than a labor issue when fewer than half of all successful representation elections lead to a first contract. And its more than some isolated, obscure labor relations issue when more than 80% of all employers facing 1991 contract expirations say they'd give thought to firing any workers who dares to use their legal right to strike." He then went on to tell what happened when in 1984, his union opened negotiations with the Canterbury Coal Company. "Its boss came to the table not with a bargaining position but only with concession demands. Dozens of demands. Take-backs on safety, pensions, wages, job security and seniority...demands that guaranteed only one thing, poverty and senseless danger for anyone who worked under them. And in August 1985, Dave Fisher and his co-workers went on strike...And each and every one of them was fired: or as the company put it, 'permanently replaced'."[11]

Also omitted by Cox was yet another factor that had a strong chilling effect on the willingness of workers and their unions to call for a strike. It was the Supreme Court decision in a 1938 case involving workers employed by the Mackay Radio Company. The Court ruled that employers had the right to hire permanent workers to replace those that went on strike. That ruling has, since the 1980s, allowed increasing number of employers to deprive their unionized workforces of the right to strike.[12]

The legal right of employers to replace striking workers with scabs has had a profoundly deterrent effect on working people's willingness to strike when negotiations with their employers failed to produce positive results. Whereas in the 1950s and the 1960s, hundreds of strikes occurred each year involving bargaining units of 1,000 or more employees, today, in contrast, strike activity has dipped to unprecedented low levels. In 1970, there were 381 strikes involving 1,000 or more workers. By 1999 there were only 17 such strikes.[13]

The relentless erosion of the living standards of working people and their quality of life at a time when the top income people are taking an increasingly greater share of the national income drew the attention of one well known liberal commentator,

"I don't need to tell you," Bill Moyers, the television journalist, told an "Inequality Matters" Conference in New York City on June 3, 2004, "that a profound transformation is occurring in America: the balance between the wealth and the common-wealth is being upended. By design. Deliberately.

"I know this sounds very like a call for class war, but that war was declared a generation ago when the financial and business class began a stealthy class war against the rest of the society and the principles of our democracy.

"Let's face the reality. If ripping off the public trust, if distributing tax breaks to the wealthy at the expense of the poor, if driving the country into deficits deliberately to starve social benefits, if requiring States to balance their budgets on the backs of the poor, if squeezing the wages of workers until the labor force resembles a nation of serfs, if this isn't class war, what is?

"It's un-American. It's unpatriotic. And it's wrong. What we need is a mass movement of people like you. Get mad, yes—there's plenty to be mad about. Then get organized and get busy. This is the fight of our lives."[14]

Chapter One

The Extent of Unemployment

The most important point to keep in mind is that the unemployment rate announced by the government is greatly understated. The real unemployment rate is far higher. It is generally twice or three times higher. Also the government always announces the unemployment rate in percentages instead of the actual millions of the unemployed. For instance, in 1997 the government told the public that the official unemployment rate was 4.9 percent, but it did not tell us that this 4.9 percent represented 6,739,000 Americans who were without a job.[1] It is this cruel fact that the government concealed from the public. And it hides these outrageously large numbers of jobless people year after year. A further point to keep in mind when looking at Graph 2 below, is the great difference between the high number of unemployed between the years 1931-1940 and the very low numbers during 1943-1945. How does one account for the great difference in those numbers?

The difference is that during the Second World War, the government poured unprecedented billions of dollars into the economy to prepare the country for war. By 1944, government expenditure on goods and services, mainly for the war effort, was seven times greater than it had been in 1939. It was this huge increase in government spending that reduced the unemployment rate from 17 percent of the labor force in 1939 to 1.2 percent in 1944.

Even more importantly, from the Second World War until the present, only the massive pouring of government money, mainly into the military, has made it possible for our economy to hold unemployment below the very high rate of the Depression years of the 1930s.

This vast and continuous financial support of the economy by the federal government can only be characterized as a total transformation of the nature of the American economy. Ever since the Second World War, only this support of the economy by the federal government has kept the economy afloat. Ever since, it has been the federal government and not the so-called "free enterprise" system that has restored and kept alive, till this very day, the limp and dying body of capitalism of the Great Depression years of the 1930s. It has been the continuing massive pouring of government money that has kept the official unemployment rates at levels lower than those of the Depression years.

The range of support provided by the federal government to prop up the misnamed 'free enterprise' system is staggering. The supports include welfare for the corporations and the rich as well as welfare for other sections of the population. But whereas in 1996, for instance, welfare support for the poor was $130 billion, welfare support for the corporations and the rich cost the country $448 billion. That means that welfare for the latter amounted to three and a half times that for the former.[2]

Let us now see what the actual unemployment rate has been during the last century. Remember that the official statistics distort the real unemployment rate, which has always been much higher. But of even greater significance, as we shall see below, the rate of underemployment has increased significantly ever since the Reagan administration mounted a vicious assault on the labor movement.

The numbers in Graph 1 give us a picture of the official unemployment rate for the years 1900-2004. Note that the year 1929 was the year of the Great Crash. In 1933, the year when the depression hit working people the hardest, one in four workers were without a job. In 1944, after three years of war, working people enjoyed the lowest unemployment rate in the twentieth century: 1.2 percent.

Graph 1.

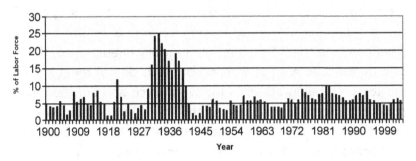

Graph 1: Official Unemployment Rate for the Years 1900-2004

Graph 2.

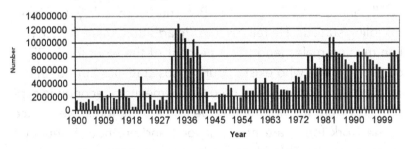

Graph 2: Official Unemployment Numbers for the Years 1900-2004

The figures in Graph 1 give us the **official** unemployment rates in percentages and Graph 2 the **official** unemployment in numbers (in millions). Though we do not have systematic numbers for the **real** unemployment rate, a number of studies have provided estimates based on a critical analysis of the government's methods of calculation.

The most recent and revealing description of the way the government distorts the unemployment rate was made by Lester Thurow, professor of economics at the Massachusetts Institute of Technology. He ridiculed the official claim that the unemployment rate in 1995 was hovering around 5.7 percent. "Even that official 5.7 percent," Professor Thurow tells us, "was 7.5 to 8 million people, hardly a small number of working people, many of whom had families to support." Thurow then went on to say that "like an iceberg that is mostly visible below the waterline, officially unemployed workers are just a small part of the total number of workers looking for work or for more work. If we combine the 7.5 to 8 million officially unemployed, the 5 to 6 million who are not working but who do not meet any of the tests for being active in the work force and are therefore not considered unemployed and the 4.5 million part time workers who would like full-time work, there are 17 to 18.5 million Americans looking for work or for more work. This brings the real unemployment to almost 14 percent."

Thus, through some wonderful voodoo recipe, the real unemployment rate of 14 percent is cooked to become the officially announced 5.7 percent. But Thurow reveals yet another troubling statistic. He tells us that "in addition, there are 5.8 million missing males (another 4 percent of the work force) 25 to 60 years of age who exist in our census statistics but not in our labor statistics. They have no obvious means of economic support. They are the right age to be in the work force, were once in the work force, are not in school, and are not old enough to have retired. They show up in neither employment nor unemployment statistics. They either have been dropped from or have dropped out of the normal working economy. Some we know as the homeless, others have disappeared into the underground economy.[3]

The government's Bureau of Labor Statistics (BLS) undercounts unemployment in several other ways. According to Michael Yates, the work of counting the unemployed is done by the Bureau of Labor Statistics and the Bureau of the Census.

Each of these government agencies, Yates says "conducts a survey of 65,000 households to figure out the national unemployment rate. To be counted as employed a person must be sixteen years or older and must have worked at least one hour a week previous to the survey. You are counted as employed whether you are a full-timer or a part-timer. Note also that you are considered employed even if you worked on Monday but were laid off on Tuesday and spent the rest of the week looking for work. Further, you are counted as employed if you worked at least fifteen hours a week without pay in a family business or have held a regular job but did not work due to illness, bad weather, temporary leave, strike, lockout, etc. Women who are home-makers but are looking for paid work are also not counted among the unemployed."

But the story does not end with the above distortions. "In addition" writes Yates "the Bureau of Statistics has made changes over the years that have further lowered the official unemployment rate. For example, since the early 1980s, the armed forces have been counted among the employed, thus further reducing the official unemployment rate. Also, in the past, people on strike were counted as unemployed if they looked for work while on strike, but now they are counted as employed for the duration of the strike."[4]

Another source reveals how the (BLS) lies about the extent of unemployment. In 1974, this source wrote, "an average of 8 million people or 6.4 percent of the work force were officially counted as unemployed. But the rate would jump to at least 9.2 percent if the BLS counted every one who wanted to work but couldn't. By undercounting in several other ways the BLS understates the economic distress suffered by millions of people. The most glaring exclusion is the category of 'discouraged workers.' These are people who are available for work and have looked for a job within the past year but have stopped searching. The BLS counted an average of 500,000 such workers in

1994. Also omitted by the BLS were 1.3 million people who said they were available for work, but were not currently looking due to family responsibilities, time taken by school or training or by health problems. Another 4.3 million said they were working part-time either because they could find only part-time work or because business was slack. By assuming they work an average half time or only four hours a day, we can incorporate these workers into the unemployment count and count half of them as unemployed. In other words half or 4.3 million equals 2,150,000. Adding together the three categories above, the number of unemployed rises to 11.9 million or 9.2 percent."[5]

Yet another category of working people not included in the government unemployment numbers are those with disabilities. In 2003, 1.3 million working-age Americans, who are limited by their disabilities but are still able to work and are actively looking for work, do not have jobs. They account for 13.5 percent of the 10 million officially unemployed workers.[6]

Why does the government undercount the unemployment rate and why does it announce that rate only in percentages? Any government administration which tolerates the cruelty of unemployment will tend to hide the immensity of the problem by hiding the total number of the unemployed. By reducing mass unemployment to a few percentage points, it hides the fact that millions of our fellow humans face serious problems.

The Rising Tide of Underemployment

A new reality has been developing since the 1980s and has accelerated since then. The new reality is that an increasing number of working people can find only part time work even though they need and would prefer to work full-time.

In 1998, the latest year for which information on the extent of underemployment is available, there were 21,000,000 peo-

ple working part-time or less than 35 hours a week. Of this number, a total of 4,686,000 people wanted full time work but were
able to find only part-time work. About 18,500,000 worked only
part-time for reasons beyond their control. These were people
who were taking care of children or had other family obliga-
tions, had health problems, were in school or training, were
retired or were constrained by the limits placed by the Social
Security Administration, and some other factors.[7]

These part-time workers are just one of several armies of
what is known as contingent workers. Other than part-timers,
these contingent workers include temporary workers, short
term contract workers and casual and day laborers. Between
1982 and 1990, temporary jobs grew ten times faster than full-
employment jobs. In 1992, two thirds of all new jobs were temporary.[8] And most recently, it was reported that temporary jobs
have nearly tripled since 1990.[9]

How fast is part-time work increasing? According to the official count, whereas in 1969 part-time workers were 15.5 percent of the work force, in 1989, part-timers accounted for 18.1
percent. And this, it should be noted, is the official rate.[10]

Who are the working people who find themselves in part time work? They are mostly teenagers, women, people of color and the elderly. But what is also quite amazing is that despite all the election campaign hype during recent election years about the importance of reforming education, many well-educated people have been compelled to take only part-time work.

As early as 1991, Jane Bryant Quinn reported that managers and professionals were the newest entrants to the involuntary contingent workforce. Quinn identified fifty firms that specialized in placing part-time managers. Many of these managers hire themselves out as executive temps who might design an information system, revise a company's accounting procedures or try to save a small company in trouble. "These part-timers," she says, "are part of thousands of superfluous middle managers who are becoming consultants or working part time solely because the jobs they once filled have been blown away." She goes on to say that "desperate executives are beating down the doors for work." One Cleveland based temp agency has more than 3,500 names – project engineers, marketing and sales managers and financial executives – in its data base, and according to that agency, it will never be able to place all of them.[11] Dwarfing all other temporary employment agencies is Manpower International, which in 2005 employed 457,000 temporary employees in the US.[11a]

Camille Colatosti writes that corporations have been telling us that workers desire part time and temporary because they are seeking more flexible arrangements and that may be true for some workers. But the real reason so many workers are forced to hop from one job to another with the inevitable jobless intervals is that employers themselves want flexible, cheap workers who are insecure enough to be more easily controlled. As part of the temporary workforce, part-time workers often receive lower wages, enjoy fewer benefits and have less job security than a company's permanent employees. The availability and the hiring of temporary workers will often allow employers to drag down the working conditions and wages of permanent employees.[12]

Yet another group of well-educated workers who have become part of the contingent workforce are teachers in American colleges and universities who were traditionally full-timers. Part time teachers now account for about 38 percent of faculty appointments. In community colleges, part timers account for as much as 52 percent of faculty. Many community colleges have only a few full time faculty, part of whose job is to organize and supervise a large number of part time teachers.[13]

Chapter Two

The Sharp Conflict of Interest Between Working People and their Employers That Preceded the Assault and Defeat By the Representatives of The Business Class of the Full Employment Law Proposal of 1945

Nearly hidden in American history have been the untiring and relentless efforts of businessmen, not as individuals but as a class, to control the working conditions of working people.

In no period of American history has the attempt of the business class to control the conditions of working people at their jobs been more dramatically evident than during the closely related series of events stretching from 1934 to 1947.

When in the very early 1930s the Great Depression hit America and millions of American workers suddenly found themselves without jobs, President Roosevelt and his advisers pushed for a solution that would alleviate the misery of the jobless. To this end the National Recovery Act (NRA) was enacted. Among the many provisions of this Act was a section designated as Section 7a. Section 7a declared that "employees shall have the right to organize and bargain collectively through representatives of their own choosing and shall be free from the interference, restraint or coercion of employers of labor, or their agents, in the designation of such representatives or in self-organization or in other concerted activities for the purpose of collective bargaining or other mutual aid or protection. No employee and no one seeking employment shall be required as a condition of employment to join any company union or to refrain from joining, organizing or assisting a labor organization of his own choosing."

Section 7a created great shock waves in the business community. For the first time in America's history, a law was enacted for the express purpose of dramatically reducing the power of business to control the working conditions of employees, while at the same time giving most workers significant advantage in bargaining with their employers about these conditions.

Businessmen now proceeded to subject Section 7a to a barrage of denunciations. The influential business journal "*The Commercial and Financial Chronicle*" called the National Industrial Recovery Act "one of the most objectionable pieces of legislation ever presented to Congress." The NRA was attacked by Lewis Brown of the Johns-Manville Company, by Charles R. Hook of the American Rolling Mills Company, by George R. Houston of the Baldwin Locomotive Company, and by eleven other durable goods magnates. These fourteen businessmen who claimed to be employing half the manufacturing force of the country, denounced the bill as inviting unions to use "without restraint or responsibility, the most dangerous weapons of social coercion." Railway magnate Henry Harriman predicted that the bill would have a "disastrous effect upon the economic life of the country." Alfred P. Sloan, Jr. of General Motors went even further. He said that if industry "has any appreciation of its obligation to future generations, it will fight this proposal to the very last." So fierce was the campaign against the bill by the National Association of Manufacturers that David Lawrence of *United States News* called it "the greatest ever conducted by industry regarding any congressional measure."[1]

Many sections of the NRA were favorable to the interests of business. What incensed and united all businessmen was the NRA's Section 7a.

American employers had worked long and hard to keep unions out of their firms. As early as 1903, the National Association of Manufacturers (NAM) had mounted a virtual "crusade" to try to wipe out unions through what was known as the Open Shop Drive. The NAM established a Citizens Industrial Association that worked with 247 employer associations to distribute anti-union literature and compile blacklists of labor activists. It also worked with the American Anti-Boycott Association, which specialized in taking unions to court. State and federal judges issued hundreds of injunctions against strikes, organizing drives and other union activities.[2]

After 1924, employers in large portions of industry created or inspired company-controlled organizations of workers. These organizations became known as company unions, and their aim was to provide a docile labor force.[3] It has been estimated that during the New Deal reform years, business formed between one and three million additional company unions. In a study of company unionism, the United States Department of Labor reported that in the industries it examined, 64 percent of all existing company unions were established during the period of the National Recovery Act.[4]

Aside from the very small proportion of workers who were members of the American Federation of Labor, the working conditions of the vast majority of working people were under the control of their employers.[5]

Although Section 7a was intended to give workers significant advantage in their relations with their employers, it had two flaws that many employers were quick to exploit. First, Section 7a lacked any mechanism to enforce its provisions. For example, it could only recommend but not compel the Justice Department to investigate any possible violation of the law. Secondly, Section 7a was ambiguous in one very important respect. While it declared that "employees have the right to organize and bargain collectively through representatives of their own choosing," it was interpreted by employers to mean that workers had the right either to stay in company-controlled unions if they were already in them, or to organize themselves into company-controlled unions.[6] As a result of that ambiguity, the boldest anti-union employers were able to resist the pro-union rulings of the National Labor Board, whose prestige became seriously damaged and whose authority was then disregarded by industrialists throughout the country.[7]

By 1933, workers had become increasingly angry at their employers' campaigns to prevent the establishment of, or to drive out, independent unions. The collapse of the economy further eroded working conditions. Numerous workers saw their already low wages cut, their working hours reduced and their work speeded up. Millions were laid off. In additions to these grievances, workers resented the almost unlimited power that foremen and supervisors held over their lives.[8]

"Often workers who had relatives or friends in management or who gave presents or kickbacks to supervisors kept their jobs while more senior employees were laid off. At the same time, many companies reduced or eliminated their benefit programs. General Electric, for example, stopped paying bonuses to workers with good attendance records, eliminated paid vacations for blue collar workers, and stopped subsidizing home mortgages."[9]

Encouraged by their new right to organize without interference by their employers and relieved of the fear of government repression, guaranteed under Section 7a, large numbers of workers joined independent unions. And when employers refused to accept, or to negotiate with, these unions, workers all over the country went on strike. The national stage became the scene of strikes on a scale never before witnessed in our history. In just one year, from mid-1933 to 1934, some 2.5 million men and women walked off their jobs.

By the end of 1935, Roosevelt and his advisers realized that business defiance and the consequent mass strikes made a sustained recovery of the economy impossible. The President, who until then had vacillated between business and labor, eventually heeded his advisers who advocated a greater balance of power between the two.

The Remedy: The Wagner Act of 1935

In June 1935, the flaws of Section 7a were corrected by the enactment of the National Labor Relations Act, also known as the Wagner Act, named after Senator Robert Wagner, a Democrat from New York, who introduced the bill into Congress. The new law granted workers the right to choose their own unions by majority vote as well as the right to strike, to boycott and to picket. Further, the law forbade employers to finance company unions, to dismiss employees advocating for worker rights, to blacklist any of their workers or to use spies against them. Elections by workers to decide who would represent them would be overseen by a National Labor Relations Board, newly set up to make sure that elections would be conducted fairly.

Thus, in 1935, for the first time in America's history, it became illegal for employers to interfere with the right of working people to join their independent unions. Employers were also barred from interfering with or dominating independent labor organizations, discriminating in the hiring or firing of workers, discharging workers for giving testimony before the National Labor Relations Board provided for in the Act and refusing to bargain collectively with the workers' elected representatives.

At one stroke, the Wagner Act outlawed the very practices long employed by businessmen and which they had previously used with impunity to suppress attempts by

workers to better their lot. Furthermore, the framers of the Act were determined to stamp out company unions set up and dominated by businessmen and their managers.[10]

Before the Wagner Act was passed, workers could vote for more than one union. They could choose between a company union and an authentic one. The new law now granted workers the right to choose their own union by majority vote. It also banned any kind of management participation in or encouragement of a company union and it forbade proportional representation which would have allowed more than one union to represent workers in any given trade or company. Union pioneers in steel, auto and electrical products as well as the authors of the Wagner Act had plenty of experience with company efforts to divide, manipulate and 'speed up' their employees. Wagner and his colleagues saw such management dominated company unions as nothing more than a corporate effort to thwart and corrupt the authentic voice of a firm's employees.[11] Now granted the right to choose the union that they thought best represented their interests, most workers now chose their own independent unions.

To fully grasp the significance of the Wagner Act, one has to understand how workers were treated before Section 7a and the Wagner Act became law. Other than the members of the American Federation of Labor, which organized a very small fraction of the nation's working people, the overwhelming majority of workers lacked any kind of protection from their employers. Because millions of workers were competing for an insufficient number of available jobs, businessmen-employers took advantage of the situation by keeping wages as low as possible, thus driving many workers and their families toward poverty and often a bare subsistence level.

Before the Great Crash of 1929, the average weekly pay of the 33 million wage earners was $25 a week. More than half of the workers fell below that average, and less than one tenth were earning as much as $40 a week. For women, the highest median wage was $16.36 a week, and the lowest, in Mississippi, was $8.29. When during the 1920s, it was said "that a golden glow shed its radiance on every man," the Brookings Institute reported that almost 60 percent of the nation's working people did not receive sufficient income to buy the basic necessities of life.[12]

In 1929, an income of $2,000 was needed by an average family to provide for the most basic necessities. But in that year, the richest year until that time in all of America's history, 16,354,000 American families or 59 percent of America's population received less than $2,000 a year. Nearly 6,000,000 families received less than $1,000 a year while 12,000,000 families or 42 percent of the population received less than $1,500 and 20,000,000 families or 71 percent received less than $2,500 a year. **On the other hand, one tenth of one percent of the families on the top received as much income as did forty two percent of the families at the bottom.**

Workers were often compelled to work many more than eight hours a day. In 1929, only 1,000,000 out of the 33,000,000 workers were on the 5-day week. In the iron and steel industries the work week was 54.6 hours, in textiles 53.4 hours and in street labor 60 hours. According to the U.S. Bureau of Labor Statistics, due to the long hours and the speed of the work process, the work place killed 25,000 workers every year, permanently disabled 100,000 and injured 3,000,000.[13]

The lot of many of the country's farmers was even worse than that of the urban workers. In 1929, the monetary income of fully half of the farmers was not much more than $350 a year.[14]

A crucial aspect of the Wagner Act was that it allowed millions of working people to stand up to the personal humiliations they had suffered at the hands of plant foremen, who represented the employers. The Wagner Act gave workers the right to some measure of integrity and dignity. How workers were treated previously may be surmised by what one Chevrolet employee in Flint later recalled. "The foremen," he said, "treated us like a bunch of coolies. 'Get it out. If you cannot get it out,' he threatened, 'there are people outside who can get it out.'"[15] And when General Motors finally recognized and agreed to negotiate with the United Auto Workers (UAW), union activists finally had the right to speak up, to recruit other workers and to complain to management without fear of retribution. The relief felt was reflected by a GM employee in St. Louis who said, "Even if we got not one damn thing out of it other than that, we at least had a right to open our mouths without fear."[16]

Even more explicit was a comment made in a UAW handbook for shop stewards. It said, "Before organization came into the plant, foremen were little tin gods in their own departments. They were accustomed to having orders accepted with no questions asked. They expected workers to enter into servile competition for their favors."[17]

To supplement the Wagner Act and in the interest of reviving the economy, in June 1938, the Roosevelt administration enacted the Fair Labor Standards Act. Wages now had to be paid at a minimum of 25 cents an hour which, over the next seven years, would increase to 40 cents an hour. Hours were reduced to a maximum of 44 a week, to be reduced over the next three years to 40 hours a week. Any time over the maximum hours would now have to be paid at the rate of time and a half.

"Almost immediately," writes Rayback, "the wages of some 300,000 persons who were receiving less than the 25 cents minimum were raised and the hours of some 1,300,000 were reduced to 44 hours. As the standards were raised over the next seven years, more and more workers were also affected."[18]

The Counterattack of Business Against
The Wagner Act

In 1937, furious at the partial loss of the total control over the working conditions of their employees, business leaders, in bold defiance of and in violation of the Wagner Act, made preparations for a massive counterattack against working people. And for this purpose, they used every weapon in their armory.

"Large corporate employers were so certain that the Wagner Act was unenforceable that they ignored the new statute and fought organizing efforts by the Unions. Indeed DuPont and Republic Steel did more than simply help fund a legal challenge to the Wagner Act. They hired scores of labor spies, fired union activists, stocked up on guns and tear gas and financed a campaign in the press and on radio against the New Deal Union idea."[19]

Businessmen used their allies in Congress to urge the conservative American Federation of Labor to accuse the newly formed progressive Committee of Industrial Organizations (CIO) of harboring members of the Communist party among its active organizers. At that time the CIO was at the forefront in the struggle to unionize workers, especially in steel, auto and other heavy industries. Business also used its almost total control of the press to turn public sentiment against the workers, accusing them of daring to shut down the factories with their many sit-down strikes in 1937, when in fact, employers refused to recognize or negotiate with the newly formed unions. When the Supreme Court annulled the pro-worker reforms pushed through by the Roosevelt administration, Roosevelt made the error of trying to change the composition of that Court by packing it with judges favorable to his reform efforts. The business-controlled press exploited that misstep by vilifying his administration and calling the President himself a dictator.[20]

The most ferocious attack mounted by business against workers occurred in May and June of 1937. In May the Committee of Industrial Organizations (CIO) attempted to organize into a union a group of 200,000 steel workers. Republic Steel Corporation "spent $50,000 to equip its private police force with an arsenal of Billy clubs, nightsticks, pistols, rifles, shotguns, tear-gas grenades and gas guns."[21]

In preparation for their attack, the steel companies also organized anti-union Citizens Alliances in each of the steel towns with the apparent purpose of forging an anti-union mood among the people of those towns.

On the afternoon of Memorial Day, 1937, an American-flag-bearing crowd of over 1,000 steel workers, their families (including children) and supporters marched to the main gate of Republic Steel on Chicago's West Side. Even though the marchers were peaceful and the city's mayor promised the union the right to picket, "the police opened fire on the crowd. As men, women and children ran for their lives, police shot the fleeing figures in the back, killing ten. Police bullets struck thirty others, including three children and permanently disabled nine others. Another 28 were hospitalized with injuries inflicted by police clubs and ax handles."[22]

The Memorial Day Massacre was followed by a whole series of similar attacks in other parts of the country. "Across the Midwest, 8 more striking workers were killed in June, another 160 were seriously wounded and many more were subjected to tear-gas and arrest. In Monroe, Michigan, Leonides McDonald, a Black union organizer working for the Steel Workers Organizing Committee (SWOC), was brutally beaten by an anti-union crowd. Afterwards, Republic Steel's private police tear-gassed union pickets and burned SWOC's Monroe headquarters. In Youngstown, Ohio, deputies shot two strikers outside Republic's gate and injured another 42 men and women. The National Guard, sent in by Ohio Governor Davey and at first welcomed by SWOC leaders, jailed all the union organizers and hundreds of it members... Ohio National Guardsmen killed and wounded dozens of strikers and jailed hundreds more..."[23]

When, during 1936-1938, workers were defending their legal right given to them by the Wagner Act, the press and radio, owned as they are today almost entirely by businessmen, mounted a vicious public relations war against them. That war was led by the two major business organizations: the National Association of Manufacturers (NAM) and the United States Chamber of Commerce (CoC).

To get some idea of the vastness of the media war against the unions, one has only to look at a 1936 report made by Harry A. Bullis of the NAM. "Its industrial Press Service sent out its publications every week to 5,300 newspapers. Its weekly cartoon service was sent to 2,000 weeklies. One of its 'comic' cartoons, "Uncle Abner Says" was sent to 309 daily papers with a total circulation of 2,000,000 readers. Daily articles, written by well-known economists, under the heading, "You and Your Nation's Affairs," appeared in 260 newspapers with a total circulation of 4,500,000. A monthly exposition of industry's viewpoint was sent to every newspaper editor in the country.

"People reading foreign language newspapers were not neglected either. A weekly press service publication, translated into German, Hungarian, Polish and Italian, was sent to newspapers with a total circulation of almost 2,500,000. NAM also sent six full page ads about the so-called "American System" and claimed that 500 newspapers carried one or more of those ads.

"NAM sent pro-business movies, which were broadcast over 220 radio stations once a week and over 176 stations twice a week. NAM also sent 1,188 programs in six languages, which were broadcast over 79 foreign language radio stations. NAM claimed that its two ten-minute films were seen by 2 million people. It sent 8 professional speakers to 70 meetings. A series of 25 leaflets were distributed to over 11,000,000 workers. Over 300,000 posters were hung on bulletin boards in factories throughout the country. Ten sound slide films were produced for showing in factories. Sixty thousand billboard ads for outdoor advertising were prepared for 1937. Over 10,000,000 copies of 7 different pamphlets were distributed to libraries, colleges, businessmen, lawyers and educators. Even more vicious, the NAM distributed thousands of copies of a booklet endorsing the Mohawk Valley strike-breaking method as well as 10,000 copies, at a later date, of the booklet called *Join the CIO and help build a Soviet America.*

"No less active in such efforts was the Unites States Chamber of Commerce. With 700,000 members, the extent of its propaganda was as wide in scope as that of the NAM."[24]

The business-dominated press succeeded in influencing a substantial part of the public against the Roosevelt administration. In the 1938 midterm congressional elections, Republicans gained 81 seats in the House of Representatives, 8 seats in the Senate and won 13 state governors' races.

Working people were about to face a severe reversal of their fortunes. Large numbers of workers had lost their jobs in the steel industry, and the economic downturn of 1937-1938, caused partly by budget cuts made by the Roosevelt administration, brought the total number of unemployed to 11 million. The CIO now also had to contend with the need of the Roosevelt administration for the goodwill of the corporations to produce the weapons for the war looming on the horizon.

Roosevelt directed Thomas Corcoran, his special adviser and campaign organizer, to "cut out this New Deal [reforms] stuff. It's tough to win a war." Corcoran later explained that, "Roosevelt had heard complaints from the people who could produce the tanks and other war stuff. As a payoff, they required an end to what they called the New Deal nonsense."[25]

Now the compelling need of the Roosevelt administration to prepare for the coming war caused a total reversal of the power relations between workers and businessmen. The latter were granted very lucrative contracts and appointed by Roosevelt to powerful positions in his administration to direct the war effort. Almost overnight, the mood, the fortunes and the reputation of businessmen, all of which had sunk just less than a decade ago to an abysmal depth, now ascended to undreamed of heights. And conversely the fortunes of labor went into a downward spiral.

Now that business had regained almost total domination of the economy, and with the federal government wanting to make sure that the corporations would produce the vast volume of arms needed for the successful conduct of the war, Congress enacted the Economic Stabilization Act. This Act froze wages for the vast majority of workers at the level of September 15, 1942. To deter workers from walking off their jobs, a new body, the War Labor Board, representing business, labor and the public, was set up. How were the workers to be deterred form striking?

"The War Labor Board gave the union leadership new rights of control over their membership. One such control, called the 'maintenance of membership,' gave union leaders the right to cancel the union membership of any worker who walked off the job during the contract period signed by the corporation and the union leaders. Thus any worker who struck was deprived of protection by the union and could lose his or her job.

"To make sure that the union leadership would abide by the contract and keep workers on the job, union leaders were rewarded with a vastly increased membership. Corporate businessmen agreed to allow all of their workers to become union members and to automatically deduct membership dues from their workers' paychecks and hand them to the unions. Those dues poured into a thriving union treasury. To further strengthen control over union leaders, the War Labor Board had the power to deny rewarded rights to any union that did not cooperate. Union leaders who called for a strike or who did not prevent their members from engaging in unofficial strikes were deemed guilty of non-cooperation.

"In spite of business and labor leaders' mutually beneficial arrangement to keep workers on the job and in unions, workers developed the technique of quick unofficial strikes independent of and even against the union leaders on a far greater scale than ever before. The number of strikes began to rise in the summer of 1942, and by 1944, the last full year of the war, more strikes took place than in any other previous year in American history."[26]

"During the forty-four months from Pearl Harbor to V-J Day, there were 14,471 strikes involving 6,774,000 strikers. In 1944 alone, 369,000 steel and iron workers, 389,000 auto workers, 363,000 other transport equipment workers and 278,000 miners were involved in strikes.[27]

"Worker unrest became even more acute immediately following the end of the war with Japan and continued through 1946. Workers walked off their jobs for a number of reasons, but most struck because their wages had been reduced. Between the spring of 1945 and the winter of 1946, the weekly wages of workers in non-war-related industries decreased by 10 percent. Workers in war-related industries lost 31 percent and were making 11 percent less spendable income than they were in 1941.

"In September," Brecher continued "the first full month after the Japanese surrender, the number of work days lost to strikes doubled." In October, one month later, it doubled again. On September 16, 43,000 oil workers struck in twenty states. On September 21, 206,000 coal miners struck to support a demand by supervisory employees for collective bargaining. Also on strike were 44,000 lumber workers in the Northwest, 70,000 truck drivers in the Midwest and 40,000 machinists in San Francisco and Oakland. To these were added a 19-day strike by East Coast dock workers, a 102-day strike by flat glass workers, and a 133-day strike by New England textile workers.

"This was followed in late 1945 and 1946 by a huge wave of strikes spread across the country. On November 21, 1945, 225,000 General Motors workers walked out when G.M. refused to settle by arbitration a demand for a 30 percent increase in wage rates without raising the prices of its autos. That 30% increase would have merely maintained the real value of the workers' incomes. In January 1946, 174,000 electrical workers, 93,000 meatpackers, and 750,000 steelworkers struck. In April 1946, 340,000 soft-coal miners struck, causing a nationwide brown-out. In May, a nation-wide strike by engineers and trainmen almost paralyzed the nation's entire commerce."[28]

"As a total of 2,970,000 workers walked out of their jobs during the first six months of 1946, the U.S. Bureau of Labor Statistics called that period 'the most concentrated period of labor-management strife in the country's history.'"[29]

Having lost a major part of its control over the working conditions of working people due to the Wagner Act, the business community became deeply concerned about the extensive strikes, both legal and wildcat, that swept over their factories – strikes that threatened a total loss of that control.

Businesses now used their war-bred wealth and power to renew their dominance over labor. And their first major step to revive that dominance was to defeat a proposed law that would guarantee a job to every working person who needed one, a major historical event which will be dealt with in the next chapter. The second major step was the enactment in 1947 of the Taft-Hartley Law, discussed in the Introduction chapter, which crippled the power of working people from the time it was enacted until today.

Chapter Three

The Assault and Defeat of the 1945 Full Employment Law Proposal by the Representatives of the Business Class

"It goes without saying that it is scarcely respectable for the rich and their mercenaries, lawyers, economists, politicians, public relations types and so on to openly proclaim their affection for unemployment, although among friends, they tend to be more candid. One requires a respectable rationale, a convenient theory that combines apparent concern about the sufferings of the unemployed with actual capacity to avoid any action realistically calculated to alter their status."

Robert Lekachman, "The Specter of Full Employment." *Harper's*, Feb. 1977, p.38. Prof. Lekachman, now deceased, was distinguished professor of Economics at the City University of New York.

One of the truly great wonders of the monopoly capitalist system is that a lot of noise is made about the decline of the work ethic. In other words, working people either do not like to work, or when they do work they perform lazily and slothfully. But in fact, the leaders who control the economic system to benefit themselves and their fellow business people have done everything in their power to deliberately create widespread and ongoing scarcity of jobs.

No doubt some people of the working class do try to avoid work when the work itself stifles the spirit, pays too little or is controlled by a mean boss or all of the above.

UE News Service

" It was drill that hole, fit that bolt, tighten that nut until I just had to get away from it all..."

But the overwhelming numbers of the unemployed must and do work if only to do something useful and to earn a living. In a later chapter, I will show how the chairmen of America's central bank and chief caretakers of the capitalist system deliberately create unemployment. For now, I will tell about a little known but highly revealing event in American history.[1]

Shortly before the end of the Second World War, some members of Congress were concerned that the impending return of millions of servicemen to civilian life and the expected cessation of the vast production of war materials would result in large-scale unemployment. So they decided that they had better do something about it.

On January 22, 1945, Senator James Murray, a Democrat from Montana, introduced a bill in Congress called the Full Employment Bill of 1945. The bill, as originally proposed, stated "that all Americans able to work and seeking work have the right to useful, remunerative, regular and full-time employment, and it is the policy of the United States [government] to assume the existence at all times of sufficient employment opportunities to enable all Americans to exercise this right."

The proposed law also stated "that in order to assist industry, agriculture, labor, and state and local governments in achieving full employment, it is the responsibility of the federal government to pursue such consistent and openly arrived at economic policies and programs as will stimulate and encourage the highest feasible levels of employment opportunities through private and non-federal investment and expenditures."

This was followed by the crucial clause: "To the extent that continuing full employment cannot otherwise be achieved, it is the further responsibility of the federal government to provide such volume of federal investment and expenditure as may be needed to assure continuing full employment."

Thus the federal government would both guarantee the right to a job and would be responsible for creating the necessary number of jobs, so that no person seeking a job would be without one.

The proposed law also called for the creation of a special group to plan the economy in such a way that the right to a job would be guaranteed. That planning group, to be supervised and directed by the President, would prepare a National Production and Employment Budget. Its job would be to estimate in advance the gross national product as well as the volume of investment and expenditures expected from both the private and public sectors. If the estimated investment and expenditure for full employment were to fall short, states, counties and/or by private companies would be encouraged to make up the deficiency. If further funding were needed, the federal government would make up the deficiency. The president was designated to determine how much money would be invested into the economy to create full employment, when this was required.[2]

The idea that the federal government should provide the necessary money to create jobs was prompted by the utter failure of unfettered private enterprise. That failure translated into an economic catastrophe for working people, enormous numbers of whom lost their jobs. When the hearings and the debate ended in the Senate, the bill (labeled S380) passed more or less in its original form. But when hearings were held in the House of Representatives (where it was labeled HR2202), the bill's opponents buried it in an avalanche of excuses, verbal tricks and deception.

Who were the opponents? They were the country's major business organizations. They were the National Association of Manufacturers (NAM), the United States Chambers of Commerce (CoC), the American Farm Bureau Federation, the Committee for Constitutional Government and the Business Council, through its Committee for Economic Development. Especially noteworthy is how, during the hearings, the opponents first expressed support for full employment and then hedged that support with all kinds of limitations.

The Opposition of the National Association of Manufacturers to Full Employment

Ira Mosher, representing NAM at the hearings on Senate Bill 380, claimed, "There is no organization in the nation more seriously or more sympathetically or more selfishly interested than we are in the maintenance of full employment. We cannot prosper unless people have jobs and can buy our goods." However, his true position on full employment became clear later in his statement, when he said, "I recognize the term [full employment] can be interpreted to mean that everyone must have a job at all times. And I am thoroughly familiar with the argument, and that the fact that such a situation can prevail only under a system of totalitarianism or under an economic system which is so poor that everyone, men and women, young and old, has to work today in order to eat tonight."[3] Mr. Mosher conveniently ignored the fact that nowhere in the proposed law was it mentioned that everyone must have a job at all times. The bill said only that "all Americans able to work and seeking work have the right" to a job.

Mr. Mosher revealed what he really thought about full employment. "As I have indicated earlier," he said, "we agree with the principle [as stated in the law proposal] that all Americans able to work and seeking work have the right to useful, remunerative, regular and full-time employment, if the word 'right' is understood to mean a moral right, not a legal right enforceable in the courts. To eliminate confusion on this question, we would prefer the principle to be stated that all Americans able to work and seeking work are entitled to an opportunity (our emphasis) for useful remunerative, regular and full-time employment."[4]

What does Mosher mean by the word opportunity? The American Heritage Dictionary of the English Language defines opportunity as "a favorable or advantageous combination of circumstances." But what happens when all too frequently no "favorable or advantageous combination of circumstances" occurs as has happened during the eleven recessions before 1945 and again during the recession of 2001 to 2003 under the administration of President George W. Bush? Neither Mosher nor, as we shall later see, the other representatives of the capitalist class, have ever bothered to ask: What are working people to do who have families to support if no job opportunities exist and their unemployment benefits run out? Further, when the economy is in a recession or a depression, what are the hordes of young people just entering the job market to do? For those young people, there isn't even the possibility of receiving unemployment compensation.

Mosher went on to argue against the creation of a federal budget to plan the economy in order to secure both the principle and practice of full employment. "The first major point we should like to make," he said, "is that NAM sees no objection in theory to the preparation of a 'national production and employment budget' as provided [in the law proposal], but it does not believe that such a budget in practice can be sufficiently accurate to provide either a timely or reliable guide for government policies."[5] What Mosher overlooked is that in starting or maintaining a business, no businessman can provide an accurate or reliable guide to ensure its success. But for Mosher, the federal government is not permitted to draw up anything less than an accurate budget even though any adverse effects of an inaccurate budget would be completely overshadowed by the enormous benefits, both economic and social, of a full employment economy.

What are we to make of Mr. Mosher's denial of the federal government's need to plan the economy? Andrew Hacker writes, "National hypocrisy has in few places as many facets as it has in the simple rhetoric of the opponents of [national] planning. The most violent anti-planners are the same men who expertly plan the future of their corporations for ten to thirty years and who rely on [their] planners to keep their suburbs from infestation by junkyards and filling stations."[6] A more pointed explanation of business opposition to federal planning for full employment was offered by David Vogel. He wrote, "The true meaning of freedom for the American bourgeoisie [the capitalist class] is the ability of those who own or control economic resources to allocate or appropriate them as they see fit – without interference from either labor unions or government officials."[7]

Arguing in favor of the pressing need for national planning, Harry Magdoff wrote: "If the economy is to be subservient to society – to serve the welfare of all the people, to eliminate poverty, underdevelopment and mass misery – then central planning is an absolute necessity. In addition, it cannot be stressed too strongly: national planning is equally essential before it is too late for the globe to remain a livable habitat for human beings. This does not necessarily mean that every detail of production and distribution should be dictated by authorities at the center. We know from bitter experience how counterproductive rigid, excessively bureaucratic planning can become. But there is no escape from the simple fact that resources are limited and choices must be made as to how they will be allocated. Basically there are two ways. Resources can be allocated via the market, where price and profits do the rationing, or they can be allocated in such a way as to most suitably meet social needs.

"The necessity for social planning was shown in the United States during the Second World War when the national priorities were crystal clear (e.g., military airplanes versus civilian autos, tanks versus home refrigerators, barracks versus civilian homes). Central planning was the only way an industrial miracle was achieved. In short order, the armaments, transportation facilities, food, clothing and housing for military forces fighting on two continents were supplied. Authorities in Washington in effect dictated what to produce (not in every detail but with sufficient direction to assure that the most urgent priorities would be met), what sort of productive capacity was to be built, and how to distribute the insufficient output of metals, industrial supplies, metal working machinery, etc."[8]

Ira Mosher's appearance before the House committee was only a small part of the campaign against full employment conducted by NAM. NAM mounted a widespread campaign to influence the public to defeat the proposed law, using radio, public meetings, news, cartoons, editorials, advertising and motion pictures to disseminate its views. NAM sent a summary of Mr. Mosher's testimony to its own membership of 16,000 and to an extensive mailing list. It also sent a one-page flyer to 2,500 columnists and editorial writers across the nation, to 7,500 weekly newspapers and to 35,000 farm leaders.

Thus NAM's activities against the Full Employment Bill of 1945 helped to mold the opinion of a large segment of the population.[9] But some of NAM's largest contributors aided its work. The most prominent was Donaldson Brown, vice chairman of General Motors Corporation and a member of NAM's board of directors. Brown recruited two staff members who worked behind the scenes to persuade Carter Monasco, Chairman of the Committee holding the House hearings, to include many more witnesses opposed to full employment. Brown's aides drew up a document virulently attacking HR2202. It declared that the bill would mean government controls, that it would destroy private enterprise, increase the powers of the executive and lead to socialism, and that it was unworkable, impractical and promised too much.

The Opposition of the Chambers of Commerce to Full Employment

Also working relentlessly to defeat the full employment bill were the country's numerous Chambers of Commerce (CoC), all of which are affiliated with the national United States Chamber of Commerce. This organization's members have generally been owners of businesses that deal mainly in the distribution and sales of products and services.

In 1945, the U.S. Chamber of Commerce was a federation of 1,700 business groups. Also affiliated with the CoC were 2,000 organizations and 15,000 business firms and corporations. Additionally, there were 135,000 individuals who belonged to the U.S., Junior Chamber of Commerce.

Although small businessmen and professionals such as shopkeepers, realtors, insurers, lawyers and bankers made up most of its membership, the Chamber's decision-makers have usually been persons connected to powerful business and banking concerns.

The Chamber of Commerce has a powerful influence on those who identify with the interests of business. Then CoC engages in a wide range of activities and functions. At its headquarters in Washington, D.C., it conducts research and makes known the views of organized business to the administrative agencies of the executive branch. Its various committees analyze issues and disseminate information to its members and to the interested public. The Chamber's publicity staff prepares news about the views of the Chamber for release to the daily press and to specialized journals. Its official organ, "Nation's Business," presents the Chamber's views to its members and to the public. During Congressional sessions, its staff follows closely the work of Congress and keeps the membership informed of legislative developments relevant to their interests.

Leading the Chamber's assault on HR2202 was Walter Spahr, a professor of economics at New York University. That businessmen feared and opposed the prospect of full employment became clear shortly after his opening statement. He said, "Should the full employment bill HR2202 become law, and should Congress and the Administration seriously attempt to make the provisions effective, the people of the United States apparently will find that something of far greater importance has happened to them than they now seem to suspect."

Spahr questioned the possibility of measuring accurately the gross national product, the aggregate volume of investment and expenditures. He even questioned the concept of regular and full-time employment. "What, for instance," he asked, "is 'regular' and 'fulltime' employment? How many days per week must one work, how many hours per day, how many adult members of the family must work, how many holidays may there be, at what age may one begin work and at what age may or must one retire?"

Spahr compared the possible results of the Bill to what occurred during the Depression years. "When a policy, much like the one proposed, was tried in the country during those years, the economy was so disturbed that unemployment remained at a high level despite the heavy government expenditures."

Spahr very conveniently forgot that the level of unemployment remained high during the Depression decade not because of the high level of government expenditure but because those expenditures were too low. According to Rexford Tugwell, assistant secretary of agriculture in Roosevelt's administration, Roosevelt tended to resist spending for fear of creating deficits. Roosevelt had therefore been unwilling to spend the necessary number of dollars for public works and other needed programs to eliminate the huge lack of jobs. According to Tugwell, "during the [first] hundred days [of Roosevelt's administration, $3.3 billion was appropriated for relief and public works. That may have seemed an astronomical figure to conservative citizens; but Senators LaFollette and Wagner who were the real experts in this matter after two years of dueling with President Hoover, Roosevelt's immediate predecessor, knew that a much more realistic sum would have been $12 billion. They were quite right, if the relief of unemployment was the true goal. Roosevelt's spending was never enough to provide everyone with purchasing power, and consequently to ensure recovery. Far more government spending would have been required. The reason spending fell short was that Roosevelt was just as convinced as Hoover had been, that unbalanced budgets were politically risky."[10]

Spahr described various aspects of the Bill as "dangerous." The danger to which he referred was the "tendency for the [government] to compete unfairly with private enterprise and to cause it to shrink and die, which in turn, provides the excuse for further expansion of government employment activities." Spahr feared that big business would lose some of its power to control the economy, if the government would intervene to provide full employment.

What Spahr may have had in mind were wage rates paid to African American workers employed by the federal government for projects such as the Tennessee Valley Authority – wages which were higher than those paid by Southern planters to their African American share-cropping tenants. Also significant is what freedom meant to Spahr and the business class he represented. "The Bill," Spahr said, "does not face the fact that an individual cannot have freedom without at the same time incurring risks. It assumes that the people of the United States have reached a stage in which they are willing to sacrifice their guarantees of freedom to obtain what is in fact a spurious guaranty of employment." Spahr's real objection to the bill followed immediately. "It [the proposed law] embodies the doctrine that every person is entitled to obtain a living from the government regardless of whether he has the ability or the willingness to produce enough to justify the pay which it is proposed that he shall have."

In other words, if every person had a right to a job, would he work hard enough to ensure profits for his employer? Why is a job spurious if guaranteed by law?

Mr. Spahr's fear is that the inadequate wages paid to numerous workers will deter them from performing well at the job and that therefore what is needed is the fear of unemployment. In other words, because the carrot offered is far from adequate, what is needed is the stick of the fear of unemployment. For, from the viewpoint of the corporate elite, without the fear of being fired, what would prod the working person to perform to the satisfaction of his employer?

Fearing that employers would have to compete with the government in providing jobs to the unemployed, Professor Spahr says, "This bill opens the way to far-reaching government action to such employment as it may see fit to provide. The government could and probably would enter many fields of activity that are not proper functions of government – if we are to maintain the system of free enterprise. Despite the great concern repeatedly expressed in the bill over the preservation and fostering of free, competitive, private enterprise, the program in its essence is a monument to a striking lack of faith in the virtues and strength of private enterprise."

How wonderful is the mind in its ability to suppress what it does not like to remember. Spahr very selectively forgot the misery inflicted on working people just ten years earlier due to the complete collapse of the free enterprise system. That his "faith in the virtues and strength of the private enterprise system" was not quite perfect was made clear in the following exchange with Congressman Cochran, one of the members of the House committee conducting the hearings on the bill.

Mr. Cochran: Do you understand that the policy laid down in the bill is that the government is to remain on the outside until it is absolutely disclosed that private industry has been unable to take care of the unemployment situation?

Mr. Spahr: As I understand it, I stated that I had studied this very carefully and I believe you have stated it accurately.

Mr. Cochran: Do you approve of advance planning?

Mr. Spahr: Do you mean, for example, in connection with a public works program?

Mr. Cochran: Yes.

Mr. Spahr: Yes. I do. I think that the federal government, if it could lay out programs for public construction when they know they are going to do these things and need these enterprises, if they can be ready to throw them into gear when unemployment becomes very pronounced, I think it would be an excellent idea.

Here Spahr admits in a roundabout way that in the private enterprise system, unemployment can become very pronounced. But why does he only **then** accept the help of the federal government? Because when unemployment became very pronounced during the depression decade of the 1930s (almost one out of four working people were unemployed), many businessmen felt threatened by the possibility of a socialist revolution and lived in a pall of fear.

Professor Spahr, who welcomed government intervention to provide jobs for workers when unemployment became "very pronounced," revealed that he was not opposed to government aid to small businesses.

Mr. Cochran: You feel that the government should leave private enterprise alone, do you, to the greatest extent that is possible?

Mr. Spahr: Of course, that opens a very big field, as you appreciate.

Mr. Cochran: Are you opposed to a small businessman now appealing to the government agencies and to the committees of Congress for help?

Mr. Spahr: That is such a broad statement that I do not think I am competent to generalize in my answer to that.

Mr. Cochran: Nevertheless, we are doing that very thing in fact. We have a small business agency set up in the executive branch. We have Small Business Committees, we have one Small Business Committee in the House and one small Business Committee in the Senate. We have small businessmen all over the country who are continually appealing to them for assistance. If this organization [the Chamber of Commerce] is opposed to this bill and to government interference, aren't they in direct contrast to what they are doing, appealing to the government agencies?

Mr. Spahr: I see what your point is. You say that we have an organization that is opposed to the bill? I am not certain that I follow just what you mean there.

Mr. Cochran: I say, if this organization that you are speaking for is opposed to this bill, then I ask you how they can come to an agency of the executive branch of the government and appeal to them for help and come to the two committees of Congress appealing for help?

Mr. Spahr: Frankly I am not in a position to answer that question.[11]

You, the reader, are invited to try to fathom the meaning of that last response.

Have the policies of the Chamber of Commerce undergone any changes since attacking and helping to defeat the full employment law proposal of 1945? In the fall of 1999, the Clinton administration proposed new rules that would have prohibited the granting of federal contracts to companies guilty of repeated and substantial violations of discrimination, labor, tax, environmental or anti-trust laws. One would think that such rules would, in the words of Molly Ivins, be as safe as supporting motherhood. Not so. The Chamber of Commerce "promptly leapt to the defense of the lawbreakers, claiming that the rules would be a 'blacklist' and a 'sop' to organized labor.

The reaction of Thomas Donahue, the Chamber's president, left no doubt. He said that "the new rules will be used principally to punish companies that have violated labor laws such as prohibiting companies from firing workers in unionization drives..." And that "he would [therefore] do whatever is necessary to block this politically motivated policy."[12]

The Opposition by the Committee for
Constitutional Government to Full Employment

Frank Gannett, Sumner Gerard, Dr. Willford King and one-time Indiana Congressman Samuel Pettergill headed the Committee for Constitutional Government. This Committee fought every bit of progressive legislation introduced by the Roosevelt administration during the thirties and forties. As early as 1943, the Committee circulated a leaflet attacking the goal of full employment, calling it a 'manifestation of sentimental humanism.'

In 1945, the Committee for Constitutional Government issued a pamphlet called, "Full Employment and Freedom in America."[13] The pamphlet contained cartoons showing bureaucrats telling workers where and at which jobs they must work. Also included in the pamphlet was a vicious article alleging that the bill's ancestry was "the Constitution of Communist Russia, and saying that, "This Russian spawn entered the womb of the National Resources Planning Board....Then Henry Agard Wallace, four senators, President Truman and Sidney Hillman ordered long pants for the child and we find sonny-boy playing around the halls of Congress." And Bailey adds that according to the author of the article, the uncles of the child were Adolf Hitler and Benito Mussolini.

The Committee, in a statement of its own in the final page of the pamphlet, exhorted its readers to "make yourself a committee of one. Arouse members of your family, your associates, fellow workers in your unions, in service clubs. Give each a copy of this bulletin. Write your Congressmen and Senators. Tell them you will never forget how they vote on these bills and will support them if they put the nation's interest above the demands of pressure groups. Distribute this pamphlet widely."[14] This pamphlet was sent to a mailing list numbering hundreds of thousands. According to Bailey, "material of this sort unquestionably stimulated a certain amount of indirect pressure against the Full Employment Bill, and of course provided additional ammunition for the Congressional opponents of the Bill.[15]

The Opposition of the American Farm Bureau Federation to Full Employment

A fourth business organization that strongly opposed the Bill was the American Farm Bureau Federation. "In order to understand the position of the Farm Bureau on S380," writes Bailey, "it is necessary to recognize two facts. One is that big agriculture is big business. Two, that regardless of the claim that it represents 830,000 farm families, the Farm Bureau hews close to the viewpoint of the big commercial farmers."[16] In other words the Farm Bureau represented then, as it does now, the interests of very large agribusinesses and not the interests of small family farmers, as we shall see.

On August 30, 1945, the Farm Bureau sent a long telegram to Senator Wagner, stating that the Farm Bureau's Board of Directors had just met in Chicago and was in definite opposition to full employment. Then at the House hearings, a long statement on the position of the Farm Bureau was presented by Edward A. O'Neal, the Bureau's president.[17] His opposition to full employment was made clear from his opening statement: "The American Farm Bureau Federation of which I am president is opposed to HR2202, the so-called (sic) Full Employment Act of 1945."[18] So fearful was this representative of big agriculture that he described the proposed Bill as "striking at the very foundation of our way of life and philosophy of government."[19]

Echoing the sentiments of Mr. Mosher of the National association of Manufacturers and Professor Spahr of the Chamber of Commerce, O'Neal said: "The American farmers are not willing to try to purchase full employment by selling our birthright of freedom for a totalitarian regime."[20]

Bur perhaps O'Neal's real motive in opposing full employment may be seen in the following statement. Referring to his support, earlier in his statement, of government-sponsored public works, he said, "It is our feeling that great care must be exercised in public works programs to be sure they will not discourage employment in private enterprise. If the government is going to pay prevailing wage rates and guarantee the worker a full-time job, what is there to stop more and more workers from seeking employment offered by the government and having less and less interest in employment by private enterprise? We feel that wage rates on relief work should be such as to encourage the individual to seek employment elsewhere rather than to remain on the public payroll. The farmers of the nation resent not being able to hire help because relief projects in the community can outbid them for labor. In the 1930s, the average wage rate for common labor in road building was about two and a half times higher than the wage rate for farm laborers."[21]

O'Neal's true concerns might have been more clearly expressed if he had said: If the federal government wishes to employ workers on public works programs such as roads, hospitals, schools, parks, etc., its wages must be substantially less than the wages offered by privately owned companies. For how can the private companies find willing and docile workers if the government public works lures them with better wages? Let's not have government-funded jobs competing with private enterprise for the labor of working people, who now have no choice but to accept any kind of work at the lowest possible wage.

By contrast, on the very same day that O'Neal's statement was presented to the House Committee, Russell Smith, the legislative secretary of the National Farmers Union, which represented family farms, urged the House Committee to approve full employment.[22]

Once again, echoing his counterparts at the National Association of Manufacturers and at the Chamber of Commerce, O'Neal admitted that private enterprise is unwilling or incapable of creating enough jobs for all who need them. "The American Farm Bureau Federation recognizes that the government has some responsibility in encouraging a high level of employment in case private enterprise is unable to do so... We believe that public works, conducted on a reasonable scale and on a sound basis, can make a contribution to our national welfare."[23] It should be noted that Mr. O'Neal talks about a "high level" of employment, never about "full employment."

Further, O'Neal said, "The Farm Bureau believes that the nation can accomplish more by encouraging individual initiative, by providing an environment in which the individual has the opportunity to advance through merit, by the government underwriting only the minimum essentials of security and not attempting to underwrite [read guarantee] the full extent of security."[24] Here, O'Neal reveals his belief that government guaranteed job security is bad for people who own businesses and need to hire workers. That kind of job security eliminates the working person's fear of being unemployed and therefore gives the employee more bargaining power for wages and benefits. No business employer would ever tolerate that!

Like his counterparts at the National Association of Manufacturers and the U.S. Chamber of Commerce, O'Neal invoked freedom to justify opposition to full employment. But what does he mean by freedom? "It is our feeling," he stated, "that it is the responsibility of government to provide an environment in which the individual has an opportunity to obtain the good things of life, but it is not the responsibility of government to ensure them to all persons. It appears to me to be ironical that promptly upon the end of the war, in the winning of which we sacrificed upon the altar of freedom the lives of so many of our fine young men, that we stand today in the halls of our nation's

Capitol debating a measure which deals so recklessly with this freedom for which so many have died. Are we going to trade our freedom, which involves some risk and also offers unlimited opportunity, for a program which offers a minimum amount of security and endangers the freedom of every individual citizen?"[25]

Freedom, as defined by these business leaders, guarantees businessmen unlimited workers willing to compete for undesirable jobs at low wages, rather than freedom for workers to chose between an undesirable, low-paying job and a government job with decent pay, benefits and working conditions.

Let us digress for a moment to the root causes of the Second World War – causes about which O'Neal and the other business representatives remain silent. Let us remember that Adolf Hitler and the Nazi party rose to power chiefly due to the unemployment of millions of German workers and the liquidation of the entire savings of the German middle class, brought on by the horrendous inflation of the German mark. Both of these developments were the consequences of the total collapse of the free enterprise system from 1929 to 1939. Recall that Hitler gained power on January 30, 1933, after almost four years of mass unemployment with its great misery for Germany's working people. What lies lurking behind all this patriotic rhetoric? What do people like O'Neal, Spahr and Mosher mean when they talk about freedom? Do they mean freedom from want, from material and financial insecurity? Do they mean freedom from humiliating dependence on charity and government welfare handouts? Do they mean freedom from the fear of not being able to support a family with integrity and dignity? When they talk about "freedom", the representatives of large agricultural businesses and nearly all other large scale manufacturers really mean freedom from governmental interference in the job market, so as to leave unhampered their control over the working conditions of their employees.

The Opposition to Full Employment by the Business Council and Its Committee for Economic Development

The Business Council was created in 1933. According to Kim McQuaid, the Council was an assembly of more than 60 chief executive officers of the largest corporations in the country. In mid-June 1945, Ralph Flanders, a top member of both the Business Council and its Committee for Economic Development, sent a letter to Senator Wagner. In his letter, Flanders started out on a positive note. He wrote that he supported federal efforts to do more to provide jobs for people in need of them, calling the right to a job a "legitimate right." Then he attached conditions, saying: "The individual has no right to a job unless he is productive, self-reliant, and energetically seeks employment. To assign the right [to a job] to individuals who do not possess these qualities is to subsidize idleness and social parasitism. The government should avoid policies that lower business confidence, which would decrease businessmen's willingness to invest."[26]

When Ralph Flanders talks about business confidence, what he means is that private enterprise does not want government policies that would give workers an alternative to a private employer, who in the absence of government-created jobs, would have to accept any conditions or any job offered by the employer no matter how inadequate for a decent standard of living.

By August 1945, Beardsley Ruml, a leading member of the Committee for Economic Development, was telling congressional committees, "that all controversial terminology like 'the right to work,' 'the assurance of employment,' and even the phrase 'full employment' should be removed from the bill so that "the greatest harmony may exist among all who believe that it is both appropriate and necessary that the federal government direct its full powers toward the goal of full employ-ment." But then to weaken the bill, Ruml said, "There is some doubt in my mind whether it is necessary or even desirable to define precisely what we mean by 'full employment.' It is a con-cept that will change from decade to decade as our ideas, with respect to the relation between work and freedom, change. A definition can hardly have any substantial practical consequence as to what is recommended or legislated under the bill. Why not leave the term 'full employment' like 'liberty' or 'justice' to stand as a goal of democratic government and to derive its specific content from the will of the people as expressed from time to time by their free institutions."[27]

In October 1945, the Business Council met to ratify a report drawn up by its Full Employment Committee and to forward it to President Truman. The report began by saying that the federal concern with full employment was both necessary and desirable. Congress, it urged, should set up a permanent Joint Economic Committee to study fundamental economic mat-ters. The report also urged the White House to remain content with a temporary ad-hoc commission to do its studying for it. After demonstrating its clear support for **studying** things, the council went on to add copious warnings against the federal government's trying **to do** anything. [our emphases] The report opposed the creation of a special budget to allow the govern-ment to provide for enough jobs for all who needed one. "We feel," said the report, "that too much reliance is placed...on [government] spending as a remedy...to our economic ills [read unemployment]. Finally, the report stated that because what was left of the original full-employment bill did not present a **coordinated program** of action, the bill was "dangerous in its implied promises." McQuaid adds 'the fact that the Commit-tee for Economic Development and the Business Council lead-ers had been trying for months to ensure that **no coordinated**

program of action would ever be passed was not, of course, mentioned.[28] [our emphases]

"What eventually happened to the Full Employment Bill of 1945" McQuaid writes, "was that the House version of the original Bill was rejected in favor of a substitute written by a southern conservative, Will Whittington. Whittington asked for and received advice from the U.S. Chamber of Commerce, the Committee for Economic Development and from a Dr. George Terborgh who was strongly against any government funding for full employment. What finally emerged was a version that eliminated the word "full" from the original full employment formula_and replaced it with the much more vague term, 'maximum employment.'" Lacking any significant support from President Truman, the Bill was thus emptied of all real content and was passed as the Employment and Production Act of 1946.[29]

In the end, the substitute bill eliminated the declaration of the right to employment opportunity, the federal responsibility for full employment, the pledge of all the federal resources, including financial means to that end, and the safeguard against international economic disorder.

Thus the promise of the original bill that would have guaranteed the right to a job for all who needed one was destroyed by the coordinated assault by the representatives of the major business groups in the country.

The following are the organizations that supported the 1945 Full Employment Bill:

The American Federation of Labor, The Railroad Labor Executive Association, The Congress of Industrial Organizations, The United Mine Workers, The American Association of Social Workers, American Jewish Congress, Americans United for World Organization, American Veterans Committee, Brotherhood of Maintenance of Way Employees, Brotherhood of Railroad Trainmen, Business Men of America, Inc., Central Council of American Rabbis, Council for Social Action of the Congregational Christian Churches, Disabled American Veterans, Hosiery Wholesalers National Association, Independent Citizens' Committee of the Arts, Sciences, and Professions, League of Women Shoppers, Methodist Federation for Social Service, National Association for the Advancement of Colored People, National Board of Young Women's Christian Association, National Catholic Welfare Conference, National Conference of Jewish Women, National Consumers League, National Council of Negro Women, National Council of Scientific, Professional, Art, and White Collar Organizations, National Council for the Social Studies, National Education Association of the United States, National Farmers Union, National Grange, National Lawyers' Guild, National Urban League, National Women's Trade Union League of America, Non-Partisan Council of Alpha Kappa Alpha, Southern Conference for Human Welfare, Synagogue Council of America, Union for Democratic Action, United Christian Council for Democracy, United Council of Church Women, United States Conference of Mayors, United Steel Workers of America.

Chapter Four

How the Capitalist Class Was Able To Scuttle the Full Employment Law Proposal of 1945

"Frankly, the whole thing would fall apart if it were not for the Federal Government's taxing, spending, subsidizing, guaranteeing, organizing, assisting, regulating and generally underwriting the flow of national income. What the Big Underwriter [the Federal Government] does is to keep Big Business in business in a big way. To state the basic American proposition as simply as possible – the major corporations organize and govern industry, the government ensures that the goods are actually produced and distributed. Despite all confusion and distortion, this is the true division of roles. The [capitalist] system does not run itself. The corporations are not able to run it by themselves. This has been clear since the Great Depression...

Up to the great 1929 watershed, the relation between the business and the financial interests and the federal government can be characterized as follows: the former took most of the land, mineral and other wealth that the latter had, used as much federal power as needed to accomplish their purposes, whether one is thinking of banking, the tariffs, credit, labor injunctions or whatever; and fought a continuingly successful campaign to make certain that no federal power existed which they did not need or could not use – that if nevertheless such power did come into exis-

tence, its effective use on behalf of other groups would be frustrated, delayed or sabotaged as much as needed."

David Bazelon: *The Paper Economy*,
pp. 229 and 231

The Depression decade 1929-1939 was a crucial turning point in the relations between the Federal Government and the capitalist class – mainly the Big Business sector of that class. Not only did President Franklin Roosevelt's policies restore a tottering capitalism; those policies, all aimed at saving it, allowed the owners of small and Big Business to regain their wealth.

What were those policies? During the early years of his Administration, Roosevelt pumped millions of dollars into a bankrupt banking system thus saving the bankers from financial oblivion. He then propped up the country's ailing industries by allowing their owners to eliminate price competition.

He then set them free to determine their own profitable price levels. He also saved the farmers, mainly those who owned large tracts of land by giving them money as a reward for not growing any crops on a part of their land, and this at a time even when millions of unemployed workers needed the unproduced food and other farm products.[1]

The recovered businessmen who, according to Harold Ickes, had just months previously "been crawling on their hands and knees begging the Roosevelt administration to save them from total financial collapse,"[2] now "poured their renewed profits into their political lobbying efforts, into their control of mass communications media and [into] their resistance to change of any sort"[3] that would ease the lives of working people, both the employed and the unemployed.

However, it was the Second World War and the massive infusion of money by the Federal government into the war economy that provided the corporations with enormous wealth and, consequently, great political power. Thirty-three corporations received over half of the $175 million in federal contracts between June 1940 and September 1944, while ten alone gained almost a third. While wages were frozen at 15 percent higher than the 1941 level, corporate profits rose 250 percent higher than the prewar level.[4] To get a better idea of how the Second World War greatly enriched the business class, we need only to look at their profits before the war and during the war. Between 1935 and 1938, the last four years before the outbreak of war in Europe, corporate profits averaged $5,270,000 a year. In 1938, the last year of the Depression, corporate profits dropped to $3,300,000. But when the Federal government started granting huge war contracts to corporations in 1939, their profits almost doubled to $6,019,000 that year and rose to $6.947,000 in 1940. In 1942, corporate profits soared to $11,141,000 and in 1943 to $12,181,000. For all the years in which the United States was at war, the average yearly profits amounted to $11,400,000 or more than 300 percent above the 1938 level.[5]

This was not the only source of wealth gained by Big Business. Some of those huge profits were due to contracts that allowed Business to transfer all research and development costs to the Federal government, which allowed Business both to increase costs and to build new industries. "This transfer of all risk to the national government but all profits to the owners of large companies and the transformation of the Federal Government into not only a supplier of guaranteed markets [for military goods] with assured minimum profits, but also as a supplier of capital was an entirely new development in the relationship between the Federal Government and the corporations."[6]

Kolko goes on to tell us that during the war years, the government constructed $417 billion worth of new industrial plants and it provided well over two thirds of all the capital for military-related industrial expansion... By the end of the war about $50 billion in surplus Federal war properties was sold to the corporations at less than a quarter of the original cost. "For the first time in United States history, concludes Kolko, "the Federal government became the provider of capital, of subsidies and of contracts on a scale previously unimaginable."[7]

So much for the slogan, "get government off our backs" repeated endlessly by the spokespersons of business.

The war resulted in yet another critically important development. It further deepened the merger of key personnel in the worlds of business and politics – a process that began after the Civil War. Hundreds of businessmen took over positions of control in awarding contracts and deciding policies.[8]

Let us now see how the vastly increased wealth of corporations translated into political power and how that power was used to defeat the Full Employment Bill of 1945.

During all the years of the Second World War, corporations and other business interests increasingly used their wealth to disseminate their political views. According to V.O. Key, the propaganda campaign launched by the business interests and aimed at influencing the minds of the American people was so "overwhelming" that it dwarfed all of their public relations activities. They deluged the popular periodicals with advertisements that extolled the merits of the "American Way" and the virtues of free enterprise. While the main purpose of business interests was to flood the media with the political philosophy of capitalism, this could only have strengthened their campaigns to mold public opinion on other issues.[9]

And, as we shall see, their propaganda efforts were crucial in sinking the Full Employment Bill of 1945.

Nowhere was business more hostile to or more intent on influencing public opinion against the right to full employment than in America's rural areas and small towns. There, businessmen had so grown in wealth and power and thus in control of their communities that the lawyer-politicians, representing those districts found it increasingly expedient not to antagonize those powerful business groups. Nor could their congressional representatives ignore the powerful influence on public opinion exerted by the radio and print media in their communities, for those media were under almost exclusive control of the business class. Of the seventy two editorial comments in fifty small town dailies and weeklies that were scrutinized by Bailey, all except five were hostile to S380.[10]

Bailey goes on to give specific examples of what he calls "coincidences" in the timing of the media assault on S380. On February 20, 1945, without acknowledging the source of their information, identical editorials attacking S380 appeared in the Zanesville (Ohio) Times-Recorder and the Cheyenne (Wyoming) *State Tribune*.

On September 7, 1945, the Clarksburg (West Virginia) *Exponent* published an editorial against S380. On September 10, 1945, the same editorial appeared in the Lima (Ohio) *News*.

On the same day, identical editorials quoting material attacking S380 prepared by the Committee for Constitutional Government, appeared in the Macon (Georgia) *Telegraph* and the Cumberland (Maryland) *Times*.

Bailey then alerts us to a number of editorials hostile to S380 that quoted representatives of the National Association of Manufacturers (NAM) and other business associations. On February 12, 1945, the Columbia (South Carolina) Record quoted Rufus Tucker of the NAM. On March 7 1945, the Jackson (Michigan) *Citizen and Patriot* Quoted Ira Mosher of the NAM.

On March 6, 1945, the Ft. Dodge (Iowa) *Messenger and Chronicle* quoted from an anti-deficit spending statement hostile to S380 published by a small group of New York businessmen called Committee for Americans.

On May 6, 1945, the Bluefield (West Virginia) *Telegraph* quoted Dr. Virgil Jordan, President of the National Industrial Conference Board.

On May 16, 1945, the Rapid City (South Dakota) Journal quoted H. W. Prentiss of the NAM.

On May 16, 1945, the Woonsocket (Rhode Island) *Call* quoted Ira Mosher's remarks in opposition to a government guarantee of full employment.[11]

Also very helpful to the attack on S380 [the 1945 Full Employment Law proposal] were the scores of hostile statements of columnists that appeared in the press of the country's large urban centers. Those statements provided additional weapons to the media of the rural and small-town districts and to their congressmen. The unrelenting propaganda of the business class eventually resulted in greater numbers of Republicans in Congress and the defeat of S380.[12]

When Franklin Roosevelt was elected to the Presidency in November 1932, the Republicans, who had been the major party of the business class, were so badly trounced by the voters that they were reduced to an impotent minority. Out of 435 representatives in the House, the Republicans captured only 117 seats, and of the 96 in the Senate, they were left with only 30 seats. But between 1942 and 1946 when their propaganda efforts deluged the media, they were able in the 1946 elections to capture a majority in both the House and the Senate. From 117 representatives in the House in 1932, they jumped up to 208 and from 36 in the Senate they jumped up to 51. Although they did not hold a majority in the House, they were able, with the help of the conservative Southern Democrats, to block many of the legislative measures proposed by the Roosevelt administration and to vote down many of its progressive measures. It was this coalition of Republicans and Southern Democrats that brought down the Full Employment Bill of 1945.

In his famous State of the Union address delivered to the nation on January 11, 1944, Roosevelt called for an Economic Bill of Rights. "We have come to a clear realization of the fact that true individual freedom cannot exist without economic security and independence. Necessitous men are not free men. People who are hungry and out of a job are the stuff of which dictatorships are made. In our day these economic truths have become accepted as self-evident. We have accepted, so to speak, a second Bill of Rights under which a new basis of security and prosperity can be established for all – regardless of station, race or creed."

In his Economic Bill of Rights, Roosevelt called for: the right to a useful and remunerative job, the right to earn enough to provide adequate food, clothing and recreation; the right of every farmer to earn a decent living, the right of every businessman to be free from unfair competition and domination by the monopolies; the right of every family to a decent home; the right to adequate medical care and good health; the right to adequate protection from the economic fears of old age, sickness, accident and unemployment and the right to a good education.

At the outbreak of the Second World War, Josephus Daniels, who was Secretary of the Navy in President Wilson's administration, told Roosevelt that Wilson had shuddered at the prospect of war in 1917. Daniels told Roosevelt that Wilson had said, "There are two reasons why I am determined to keep out of war if possible. The first is that I cannot bring myself to send into the terrible struggle the sons of anxious mothers, many of whom would never return home.

"The second is that if we enter this war the great interests which control steel, oil, shipping, munitions factories and mines will of necessity become dominant factors, and when the war is over, our government will be in their hands. We have been trying and succeeding to a large extent to unhorse government by privilege. If we go into this war, all we have gained will be lost and neither you nor I will live long enough to see our country wrested from the control of monopoly."[13]

Daniels then went on to tell Roosevelt that "If our country should be drawn into this maelstrom, the benefit of your reform measures will be lost and our country will again fall into the same quagmire witnessed in 1921-1933."

What developed during and after that war was what Daniels had predicted. For among the rights that Roosevelt called for in his Economic Bill of Rights, the right to a useful and remunerative job was scuttled by representatives of both Big and Small Business and by their Congressional allies.

Chapter Five

The Opposition of the Business Class to the 1978 Humphrey-Hawkins Full Employment Bill, the Testimony of the Bill's Most Prominent Supporters and the Early Burial by the Congressional Allies of Business of Five Full Employment Laws Proposed from 1985-1999

In the latter half of the 1970s, when another attempt was made at making full employment the law of the land, it was again attacked and defeated by the representatives of the major business organizations. A full employment bill, proposed by Senator Hubert Humphrey and Congressman Augustus Hawkins, was introduced in Congress in 1974. The bill's purpose was to guarantee a job to all adults able and willing to work at what the bill called "fair" rates of compensation. The most important part of the bill was that every adult able and willing to work would actually have an enforceable legal right to a job. Such persons were entitled to sue the government for redress.

The bill also stated that if the private sector could not provide enough jobs, they were to be created by money to be provided by the federal government. Planning councils in each local community would develop private and public projects to meet community needs.[1]

The jobs that were to be created would meet a variety of urgent social needs such as housing, child care, mass transit, conservation of natural resources, the development of cultural and recreational activities and education for any one who desired it.

Why Was the Bill Introduced at This Time?

The depression of 1974-1975 added millions of working people to the unemployment rolls. Much like the major cause of the Great Depression, that of the 1974-1975 depression was the unprecedented shift of income from working people to the owners of capital.[2] That shift was made worse by the high prices charged by Big Business to consumers – mostly working people – for goods and services, even though demand for those goods and services actually declined. Consumers paid 12 percent more for their purchases in 1974 and about 18 percent more in 1975 than they paid in 1973. It was at this time that Big Business perfected its control of the prices consumers paid for their goods and services by manipulating supply and demand of their goods and services.

The Path of the Equal Opportunity and Full Employment Act of 1974 (S50)

From the time that the Humphrey-Hawkins Bill, S50, was introduced in Congress, its opponents subjected it to a gauntlet of amendments. It went through four versions and when, in 1978, it finally became law, it was but a faint shadow of its first version.

By March 1976, the original provision of a guaranteed right to a job was weakened by eliminating the right to sue. Gone was the absolute guarantee of a job for every American able and willing to work, and gone also were the provisions that would allow the government to create jobs.[3]

By the time the fourth version was enacted into law, it "had no impact on economic policies and its goals have been ignored.[4]

The failure of S50 was due not only to the business class with its incessant and relentless opposition to any kind of full employment but also to the lukewarm or conditional support by many Democrats, including President Carter himself. Many economists who held top jobs in the Carter administration opposed the bill. The most vocal was Charles Schultze, who was Carter's chairman of the Council of Economic Advisers.

Schultze believed that increasing jobs near full employment would accelerate inflation. In his testimony before Congress, Schultze said "every time we push the rate of unemployment towards acceptable low levels...we set off a new inflation. And in turn, both the political and economic consequences of inflation make it impossible to achieve full employment, or once having achieved it, to keep the economy there...Once the overall rate of unemployment edges below 5.5 percent or so and the rate of adult unemployment gets much below 4.5 percent, inflation will begin to accelerate."[5]

The Assault by the Representatives of the Business Class Against the Full Employment and Balanced Growth Bill of 1974 (S50)

When hearings on S50 were held in Congress, every large business organization sent a clear message of opposition to it as they did previously against the Full Employment Bill of 1945. But this time the main argument they put forward was that anything close to full employment would cause unacceptable inflation.

The Statement by Mr. Lewis W. Foy, Representative of the Business Roundtable

Mr. Foy presented four arguments against S50. He argued that the four percent unemployment rate, specified in the bill as being acceptable in the short term, was too low. Instead, quoting R.A. Gordon, a University of California economist, he called for an unemployment rate of five and a half percent, which he claimed was the lowest level of unemployment that would avoid creating inflation. What this meant of course was that the major business groups wanted a much larger number of jobless workers than the supporters of the bill would allow.

The second argument he presented was that the method used in compiling the statistics on unemployment was not reliable. He said that as a result of a recommendation by a committee headed by the same Professor Gordon, the method used in counting the unemployed changed in 1967, thus implying that the previous method had overcounted the number of unemployed.

Another view of the method of counting the unemployed was provided by Bertram Grossman, who at this time served as distinguished professor of urban affairs and planning at Hunter College of the City University of New York. Not without a bit of outrage he wrote:

"The knowledge elite has made fantastic progress over the past thirty years in the dubious art of undercounting the unemployed. This remarkable statistical game operates at many levels. At one level, they have defined full employment as a 'tolerable' level of unemployed first to two, [then to] three and [then to] four percent of a narrowly defined labor force and then narrowing still further the definition of the labor force and raising the level of 'toleration' to five and [then to] six percent." They have "kept from public opinion the government's findings that four to five percent of officially defined unemployment in any average month means that fifteen to sixteen percent of the labor force is officially unemployed at some time during the year." They have also "kept from the public's attention the government's findings that of the adults not in the labor force, there are **more** people not working who 'want work now' than those who are certified job seekers [those who actually fill out claims for unemployment compensation]. They pretend that most people on relief do not want to work and that they have to be forced to accept **non-existent positions at decent wages.** [our emphasis] They refuse to allow any serious survey of the work capabilities and desires of all those in the country's potential labor supply with all that this means for the continuing undercount of the 'keep-outs' the 'push-outs and the 'drop-outs' from the so called labor force."

Referring perhaps to the committee headed by Professor Gordon, he said "they have appointed a new statistical commission to cover up past cover-ups and they respond to the wave of recent criticisms by developing new ways of hiding unemployment and using the words 'full employment' to disguise the waste of human resources."[6]

Mr. Foy argued that the bill's proposal to reduce the full employment rate from 4.7 percent to 4 percent by creating public sector jobs would cost the federal government about $6.2 billion annually, more than doubling the existing public jobs creation program which, in his words, was "already large and costly." However, Mr. Foy left out the enormous economic costs of mass unemployment. About the economic costs of mass unemployment Leon Keyserling, who was asked by President Truman to help draft the Unemployment Bill of 1945, wrote as follows about the economic costs of mass unemployment: "From 1953 to 1979 we have forfeited $7.1 trillion in 1978 dollars in gross national product and 80.8 million years of civilian employment opportunities, and consequently about $1.8 trillion in public revenues at all levels, with severe neglect of national priorities and chronically rising federal budget deficits."[7]

Finally, although the bill proposed that the President would be allowed to recommend a revision of the 4 percent unemployment goal if he found that it could not be met, Mr. Foy argued that this provision would not give the President the flexibility claimed by the bill. It would rather confront him with a "no-win" situation. Either he would have to modify the goals and suffer the political consequences or, by law, he would have to present a budget and economic plan that would meet the goal. What apparently worried Mr. Foy was that "once national goals are fixed in legislation, they become absolute political imperatives and can only be reversed at great political peril" [to any Administration daring to change or reverse such goals.][8]

Perhaps Mr. Foy was really only expressing the fears of businessmen to full employment, because full employment threatened to weaken the power of the business class. Laws such as social security, unemployment compensation and the Wagner Act, which, for the first time in American history, allowed workers to unionize, increased the rights and power of the working class. None of these laws had been popular with the business class, because they gave workers more power in their negotiations with their employers. In fact, when the Roosevelt administration enacted those laws, it gained the enmity of most of the employer class.[9] And when, some years after the Second World War, the Congressional representatives of the business class dominated Congress and the Executive, they wasted no time in undoing the Wagner Act by enacting the Taft-Hartley Act which robbed workers of most of their power.[10]

The Statement by Mr. George Hagedorn, Representative of the National Association of Manufacturers (NAM)

In his written statement to the Congressional Committee conducting the hearings on S5O, Mr. Hagedorn repeated most of the arguments made by Mr. Foy. What was new in his statement was his fear that "the proposed new legislation...threatens to lock us into a new rigidity."[11] What employers feared by a "new rigidity" was any impingement on their freedom to buy and sell at whatever price they deemed appropriate, to produce whatever they wanted, to hire and fire workers whenever it suited them, and to pay them as low a wage as circumstances permitted.

Hagerdorn also argued that four percent unemployment would be so low that it would create inflation. He said further that the "safe" rate of unemployment, the "lowest rate that does not set off an accelerating inflation lies in the range of five and a half percent... In this light the four percent unemployment rate set forth in the Act is entirely unrealistic."[12] He said that four percent unemployment was not compatible with price stability and that, "Therefore we must urge Congress not [to] enact S50 or any variant form of the same legislation."[13]

Statement by Dr. Jack Carlson, Representative of the U.S. Chamber of Commerce (CoC)

In his presentation to the Congressional committee conducting the hearings on S50, Dr. Jack Carlson stated that although the National CoC is unable to support the bill, it "identified with the broad economic objectives of the bill to promote free enterprise, purchasing power, price stability and high rates of capital formation."[14] But then he supported a five and a half percent unemployment rate, citing Charles Schultze, Chairman of President Carter's Council of Economic Advisers, who had testified two years earlier that five and a half percent unemployment rate would stabilize inflation.[15]

Dr. Carlson's real concern for the 72,000 members of the CoC became apparent when he argued against the creation of government-subsidized jobs. He said that if such jobs provided wages greater than those paid by capitalist employers, it would be "a mistake." He said that workers in a "fully productive job that would pay less would in effect be enticed to go into a less productive job – one that would be financed or subsidized by the government."[16]

The statements of the representatives of business against anything approximating full employment were refuted by a number of supporters of the bill. What follows are the arguments of some of its more prominent advocates.

The Response of the Supporters of S50

Testimony of Mr. Murray Finley, President of the Amalgamated Clothing and Textile Workers Union

In response to the argument that S50 was no longer needed because the government-reported jobless rate had meanwhile receded, Mr. Finley said, "The December 1977 decline in unemployment was small consolation to the approximately six million Americans still then seeking work and could not find it. Neither would it feed and clothe the families of the more than one million discouraged workers who had given up the search for jobs out of frustration. Nor would it put an end to the problem of more than three million persons who desire full time work but cannot obtain it..."[17]

"Last year," Finley said, "more than 20 million Americans were jobless at some point and more than one third of the American people experienced unemployment in their own families." To refute the claim that high joblessness was confined to a few groups of so-called "new entrants" into the labor force: Blacks, Hispanics, women and young people, and that their joblessness was therefore less serious or pressing than that of others, he said, "These new entrants enter the job market in most cases to provide essential income to support themselves and their families... Most women work because they have to as head of households or as second wage earners in families struggling to make ends meet."

"In 1975," Finley said, "42 percent of women workers were single, widowed, separated or divorced and needed to support themselves and their dependents. In addition 28 percent were married to men who earned less than $10,000 a year. New entrants were not seeking work to escape boredom, but to escape dependency or poverty. To minimize their need for jobs and income is callous indeed... The prospect of a generation of young people brought up in idleness, dependency and without skills or work habits ought to jar some of the commentators out of their complacency... It is worth pointing out that in the fourth quarter of 1977, three out of four persons out of work were white, more than half were men and 75 percent of the jobless were 20 years of age or older."[18]

In response to the claim by the bill's opponents that inflation could only be avoided by maintaining a high level of unemployment, Finley said, "If that is so, then millions of our citizens must be asking just what kind of a system it is that depends on the idleness [of millions] for its success."[19]

In refuting the claim that near full employment causes money and price inflation, Mr. Finley said that the "simultaneous experience of high inflation and high unemployment over the past three years would seem to demonstrate the inadequacy of the 'tradeoff theory' [the theory that low inflation depends on high unemployment], "We know," he said, "that there are multiple causes of our recent inflation and those include supply shortages, lack of real competition, rising costs of housing, medical care and food and huge increases in the cost of energy. In fact, the lower production and high unemployment of the recent recession has probably contributed to inflation through lower productivity... A government that fights inflation with the jobs of its people demonstrates moral bankruptcy and appalling economic judgment."[20]

Countering the third contention of the bill's opponents that efforts to reach full employment would prove too costly and burdensome for the federal government, Finley said that, "Although it is clear that an effective national policy to achieve full employment will have significant short-term costs, it is the only effective strategy to contain the long term costs of high unemployment, lost production and higher government deficits... It has been estimated that our economy has lost $4.4 trillion in gross national product as a result of unemployment over the past 20 years. The reality is that no factor is contributing more to the federal budget deficits and the national debt [and thus to inflation] than persistent high unemployment."[21]

Finley also asked, "How does one calculate the costs of a generation of minority youth who cannot obtain work and who grow accustomed to a life of dependency and idleness? We cannot ignore the overwhelming costs of inaction with its lost production, increased social spending, lower productivity, social strife and human waste."[22]

Testimony of Coretta Scott King, Widow of Martin Luther King and a Cosponsor of S50

In her appearance before the Congressional Committee conducting the hearings on S50, Coretta Scott King expressed enthusiastic support for full employment. She said, "Massive unemployment represents the most serious threat to human dignity in our nation. It undermines our witness to human rights around the world and our confidence of our people at home. It also represents the greatest moral and social failure in our national life...[23] Joblessness is a cancer eating away at the black community, destroying our hopes, our aspirations and even our youth. But joblessness threatens far more than black Americans. In fact most of the unemployed in this country are whites. In addition, all Americans, with or without jobs, suffer the consequences of high joblessness – the lost production, the increased spending [on welfare, unemployment compensation etc.], the reduced revenues and the wasted talents and human lives."[24]

"Today," she said, "more than six million Americans are officially looking for work and cannot find jobs. Many more have given up hope of finding employment and are not even counted in government statistics. And while the tragedy...is hitting all Americans, the burden is falling most heavily on the least protected and most vulnerable members of our society – the poor, blacks, Hispanics, women and youth...Joblessness creates genuine anxiety about the future. It undermines confidence. It strains marriages. It makes family life more difficult. It adds intolerable burdens to the everyday worries of human life: How are we going to pay the doctor? How long can I hold on to my house? What do my kids think about me? What are the neighbors saying? Is there something wrong with me?

"These pressures are hard to imagine for those who are working. But they take an enormous toll on human relationships, mental and physical health and feelings of self esteem. Unemployment destroys hopes and dreams. It leads to increased crimes, alcoholism, drug abuse, mental illness and even suicide.

"In many inner-city neighborhoods, the social fabric has been destroyed by a cycle of poverty fed by recurrent joblessness. Racial and ethnic tensions are intensified. A scapegoat mentality develops in which workers blame aliens, women, minorities or young people for the loss of their jobs. Many communities are caught in an impossible squeeze with increased financial assistance and social services required by the jobless even while revenues are reduced through a loss of taxpayers."[25]

Refuting the claim by opponents of the bill that government financed jobs in the public sector are necessarily less productive, efficient or useful than employment in the private sector, Mrs. King said that the kind of jobs outlined in S50 would help to meet the vital needs of our people in housing, transportation, education, recreation and health care. "We cannot accept the notion," she said, "that a nurse's aid in a general hospital or a public service employee rehabilitating homes in our cities is somewhat less productive or contributes less than those in the private sector who sell products or work in a factory."[26]

In trying to assure business that S50 was not intended to harm their interests, Mrs. King said "the vast majority [of the jobless] will and should be employed in the private sector and the major focus of economic policy ought to be efforts to stimulate and increase private employment." But, she added, that in times of major joblessness when business could not or would not create enough jobs, "We should not exclude the essential role of public service employment. It would be far better to spend funds to create and maintain employment than to require families to subsist on unemployment compensation and other forms of assistance."[27]

S50 was supported by numerous organizations and individuals. Among those who provided important arguments to the congressional committee presiding over the hearings were Rudy Oswald, Director of Research, AFL-CIO and Irving Bluestone, Vice President, United Automobile Workers. Another prominent supporter was Michael Harrington, National Chair of the Democratic Socialist Organizing Committee. Other supporters included all the industrial unions and the major service unions, the National Association for the Advancement of Colored People, the National Urban League, Catholic and Jewish religious associations, the National Farmers Union, major women's and environmental associations, student, senior, Native American, ethnic and teacher groups, the U.S. Conference of Mayors and many others concerned about the lives of the millions of the unemployed.

In the end, gone from the original version of the Act was the absolute guarantee of a job for every American able and willing to work. Also gone were the provisions that would allow the government to create jobs. Even worse, the final enacted version made it clear that its adoption had been a hollow victory for its supporters. "From the start, writes a chronicler of the Act, it had no apparent impact on economic policies and its goals have been ignored with impunity."[28]

The Early Burial by Congressional Allies of Business of Five Full Employment Law Proposals Made Between 1985 and 1999

So concerned were members of the Congressional House of Representatives with the outrageous consequences of mass unemployment, especially among the citizens of their districts, that between 1985 and 1999, no less than five attempts were made to make full or nearly full employment the law of the land.

Of the five attempts, only the first was even allowed hearings in public. However, none of the five was even allowed to reach the point where it could at least have been debated in the full House or the Senate. They were voted against or blocked by various House committees chaired either by indifferent Democrats or inimical Republicans.

The first attempt, called The Income and Jobs Action Act, was introduced in 1985 by Congressman Charles Hayes, and was supported by sixty-six other House Democrats. Even though public hearings on the Bill were held in four different cities, the hearings had no impact on the resolve of the majority in Congress to as much as hold a debate. Thus the Income and Jobs Action Act was buried in its infancy.

The second attempt to introduce a full employment law was introduced in March 1989 by Congressman Major Owens of New York. Owens proposed a daring amendment to the Constitution, calling for the U.S. government to guarantee to each person the right to a job. This proposal failed to gain a single co-sponsor. It received neither public hearings nor debate. According to one House representative, "there is much hesitation by [Congressional] members to approve such legislation because they take amending the Constitution very seriously."[29]

Congressman Ron Dellums of Oakland, California, introduced the third proposal for guaranteed employment on October 6, 1994. It gained only eleven co-sponsors but neither hearings nor debates.

The fourth proposal, HR1591, was introduced by Congressman Matthew Martinez on May 9, 1995 and had thirty-one co-sponsors, but it too just barely saw the light of day before it expired.

Congresswoman Barbara Lee of Oakland, California, intro-duced the fifth proposal, H.R.1050, on March 10, 1999. Though it had forty-four co-sponsors, it too was denied a hearing and a debate.

It may be asked why did such attempts at creating full em-ployment fail to become law? One explanation is that there is very little public support for such laws. Another explanation is that during the years when those laws were proposed, many people believed that permanent unemployment or underem-ployment was a problem affecting only the underclass and spe-cifically the African American underclass. The so-called "culture of poverty" school of thought prominent in the 1960s contend-ed that the attitudes of the poor and not social and economic conditions were responsible for unemployment. That attitude served to isolate the problem of unemployment.

There is perhaps another explanation. What if many if not most of the Democratic members of Congress were to go out and galvanize their natural constituents, both actual and poten-tial, by preaching the many terrible consequences of mass un-employment and the great benefits of full employment? Would there still be the poor public interest and support for full em-ployment?

Chapter Six

Why Are Capitalists as a Class opposed to Full Employment?

As a class, American's business community has always been threatened by the prospect of full employment and has always opposed it for a number of reasons. What are those reasons and how do they serve the interests of business?

When masses of working people are unemployed and compete for the available jobs, business people take advantage by offering the lowest wages acceptable to the applicants, subject always to the level of skill and other qualifications required by the job. Some employers even pay below the minimum required by law, as in many of the apparel sweatshops in our large urban areas.

To better understand how mass unemployment keeps wages and salaries low, let us imagine a world in which every person capable and willing to work is employed full time. How would business people find workers if they wished to open a new business, or to expand one?[1] The only way they could find them would be by luring them away from other employers. In such a world, if many businesses were trying to find employees, the workers would have greater power to bargain for better wages and working conditions.

Mass unemployment, on the other hand, confers many benefits to the employers. When working people know that there are millions of unemployed workers from whose ranks they could easily be replaced, they are more likely to agree to work harder and demand less, as well as discouraging them from asking for a raise and from demanding improvements in their working conditions.

Furthermore, when large numbers of workers are unemployed, businesses can and do recruit strikebreakers from among the unemployed. When this happens, the striking workers are often discouraged and settle for terms either less or worse than for those for which they struck.

The business community also uses high rates of unemployment to divide the working class. They do this by using their privately owned mainstream media to turn public opinion against the unemployed workers who apply for and receive welfare benefits many of whom may be members of minority groups. The media label welfare recipients as lazy, unwilling to work, and content to live at the expense of hard-working taxpayers. Employed tax-paying workers, many of whom work at jobs that provide very little or no personal fulfillment, resent the so-called freeloaders and turn their frustrations against them. A divided working class can thus never achieve their real common rights and goals because it does not have the strength of numbers to demand better working conditions, either in day-to-day struggles or on election day.

Mass unemployment provides yet another benefit for business people. During periods of economic expansion, when more workers are needed, business is able to recruit workers from the pool of the unemployed to fill their needs. During periods of economic downturn, large numbers of the unemployed help to keep the work force submissive.

Furthermore, unemployment often tames the unions and discourages them from making wage demands. "Business periodicals have been noting with unconcealed gratification that last year's [1976] contract settlements between major unions and large corporations were considerably less expensive to employers than those of 1975 even though union members were steadily losing ground to inflation."[2] Another instance of the taming of unions was caused by the mass unemployment deliberately created in 1981 by the first Reagan administration. At that time, seven major airline companies succeeded in pressuring some 52,000 employees to accept work rules to "enhance productivity as well as wage freezes and cuts of up to ten percent." The major rubber companies, Goodyear, Firestone, Goodrich, Uniroyal and others confronted some 19,200 of their employees with threats of plants closings and thus gained changes in work rules and some wage cuts at 23 tire and non-tire plants. Some steel companies pressured 3,500 employees to accept wage cuts at three plants. At least 30 trucking companies cut the wages of their employees up to 15% and imposed more flexible work rules.[3]

There is yet another benefit that mass unemployment confers to business. When many of the sons and daughters of low income working people find it difficult to find jobs, they are more easily recruited for the armed forces whose recruiters entice them with money for a college education and other incentives. Many of these recruits are then sent overseas to protect or to expand the economic interests of some sectors of Big Business wherever and whenever those interests are threatened.

Business people oppose full employment because "they are fearful of the social and political changes it would cause – changes that could threaten their interests. The right of an employer to fire an employee would cease to play its role as a disciplinary measure. The social position of the boss would be undermined and the self-assurance and class consciousness of the working class would grow thus encouraging struggles for wage increases and ... improvement of working conditions. This would lead to instability in the work place and political unrest intensely undesirable for business. **Full employment would give more workers the wages needed to buy the foods and services owned by business people and thus would provide the latter with increased profits but business people prefer their control over the working conditions of workers produced by the fear of unemployment."[4]**

There are yet other advantages mass unemployment provides to businessmen. "Hard hit by unemployment the hunger of communities and regions for jobs and tax revenues has allowed large corporations to extort an endless assortment of valuable concessions from local and state governments, either as blackmail to keep existing installations or as bribes to lure new ones. If full employment were to materialize, it would lift the burdens of apprehension and apathy from the psyches of ordinary folk and – who knows? They might entertain radical thoughts of inviting the rich to share more of their capital gains and inheritances." There would be many benefits for working people if we did have full employment. "Employers would have to pay higher wages and in so doing the distribution of income would become more equitable. Full employment would suck into the labor force men and women who struggle on welfare, food stamps, social security, and unemployment compensation. It would push up the wages of low-paid workers whose position is scarcely less precarious than that of the unemployed. It would be a special boon to African-Americans, Hispanics, teenagers, and women – people who are last hired and first fired in expansions and recession alike. A long spell of full employment would substantially narrow existing wide differentials between the earnings of these groups and those of (the more privileged) white males. In a time of [mass] layoffs and business contraction, affirmative action is a mockery, but when there is full employment, the cry for justice is heard more sympathetically by members of the [white male] majority, whose own security is not threatened."[5]

"In a world where there are millions of unemployed and underemployed workers, firms do not have to pay efficiency wages. The same degree of cooperation, commitment, and effort [from workers] can be achieved by the simple expedient of using fear as the motivation factor. In the last five years [1990-1995], examples abound of profitable firms that simply marched in and dramatically lowered the wages of their existing workforces by 20 to 40 percent. Workers complain, but they don't quit."[6]

The consequences of mass unemployment for working people were best summarized by a trio of French sociologists:

"There's the indisputable relationship between the rate of unemployment and the rate of profit. The phenomena are not only concomitant – while some get rich in their sleep, others are every day driven further into poverty – but inter-dependent. When the stock market rejoices, the unemployed pay. The enrichment of some is in part tied to the impoverishment of others. Mass unemployment remains the most powerful weapon employers possess to lower wages or freeze them, to speed up work and degrade conditions, to make jobs precarious and the work force "flexible," to introduce new forms of domination on the job and to dismantle workplace regulations. When companies lay people off, in one of those restructuring sensationalized by the media, their stocks skyrocket..."[7]

Chapter 5

Introduction to Chapters 7-12

The absence of any federal statute that would make full employment the law of the land allows nearly all employers unfettered freedom to hire and fire their employees, barring those under unionized contracts, whenever it suits them. Thus employers have taken every opportunity to displace workers by introducing advanced technology into their manufacturing and service industries, by taking jobs to countries where labor is cheap and unprotected, by merging with other companies, by importing cheap labor and hiring illegal immigrants and by using the Federal Reserve Bank to increase interest rates whenever the high employment rates emboldens workers to bargain for better conditions. All of these ways by which the capitalist class maintains and increases its profits will be told in the following chapters.

Chapter Seven

The Great Inequality in Wealth and Income As A Cause of Mass Unemployment

During the last three decades, income and wealth inequality has increased to an extent unimaginable by any standards of justice. This chapter will attempt to trace the growth of that inequality. It will show that over the last three decades, the rich have become wealthy beyond reason and have done so at the expense of both the middle and lower income groups. It will then point to the causes of this redistribution of wealth from the middle and lower income groups to the rich. Finally I will show how this rising inequality contributes to mass unemployment.

The Rising Inequality in Income and Wealth

First is the need to understand the difference between income and wealth. Wealth refers to the assets people possess such as homes, cars stocks, bonds etc. Income is the money that people receive in a given amount of time such as wages, salaries, profits, interest receipts, social security, welfare, pensions, etc. Wealth and income are of course connected, but a highly unequal distribution of income tends to go along with a highly unequal distribution of wealth.[1]

Even before Ronald Reagan began his administration in January 1981, the real income of working people had already shrunk by 10.1 percent.[2] Reagan's administration deliberately created an unemployment rate of 10.7 percent. By December

1981 more than 25,000,000 became jobless for periods that were short for some and long for many. Unemployment of that magnitude struck a staggering blow to the income and living standards of working people.[3]

A 1984 Congressional Budget Office study showed that as a direct result of Reagan's enormous tax cuts and other give-aways to business and due to his other budgetary policies all of which were supported by the Republican dominated Congress, families with incomes below $10,000 would lose a total of $23 billion between 1983 and 1985, while the 1.4 percent of families with incomes above $80,000 would gain $35 billion.[4]

In his book, *The Politics of Rich and Poor*, Kevin Phillips writes that by 1986, the top 20 percent of families had 54.4 percent of all income, while the bottom 20 percent of families had 1 percent, and the next 20 percent had 7.6 percent. Between 1977 and 1988, while the top 10 percent of households owned 68 percent of the nation's wealth, the average family income of the lowest 10 percent declined 14.8 percent. So while the lowest 40 percent of income earners were struggling to maintain a meager standard of living, the number of billionaires doubled from 26 in 1981 to 52 in 1988. Also, between 1982 and 1988 the net worth of the 400 richest families almost tripled. Chief Executive Officers averaged a 48 percent rise in compensation in 1987 and 14 percent more in 1988. Whereas in 1979, CEOs made 29 times the income of the average factory worker, in 1988, they made 93 times more.

From 1988 to 1994, pay for private sector employees fell again, this time by 4 percent, with blue-collar wages suffering most. Wages for white-collar workers remained below the 1990 level and well below that of 1988. Despite much misleading hype, the Bureau of Labor Statistics reported a continuing shift [of workers] to lower wage industries, noting that the over-whelming majority are in lower paid service industries. What this meant was that income inequality sharply increased, with the majority of workers suffering reductions in absolute income, working conditions and social status.[5]

In its April 1994 annual review, the pro-business Fortune magazine did not hide its jubilation when it reported that the 500 most important corporations posted dazzling profits despite virtually stagnant sales growth. "Hats off, it was a heck of a year," beamed the headline of a Fortune article. And this was during a year when the so-called New Democrats of the Clinton administration were leading the country.[6]

As further evidence of the widening gap between the very rich and most working people, the Statistics of Income Bulletin of the Internal Revenue Service reported that whereas in 1981, 15,000 taxpayers each with gross incomes of more than $1 million had a combined income of $11 billion, by 1988, 65,000 taxpayers each had incomes of more than $4 million, and their combined income amounted to $173 billion. That was 16 times more that in 1981. On the other hand, the combined income of the lowest third of taxpayers declined by 24 percent. Thus in 1988, the combined income of the 36 million taxpayers with incomes under $11,000 was $155 billion, considerably less than that of the 65,000 wealthiest taxpayers who had a combined income of $173 billion![7]

By 1997, wealth inequality grew even sharper. The top 5% of households received 17% of total income in the 1970s. But by 1997, they received 21% of total income. However, this data does not provide the whole picture of income inequality because it does not include income from dividends and capital gains from stocks.

The wealthiest 25% of the Americans owned 82% of all stocks while 71% of households owned no shares at all or held less than $2,000 worth in any form.[8]

" I know it isn't much, but my boss lets me
peek at his Wall St. Investor's Tip Sheet..."

The Census Bureau reported that the top half of 1% of households increased their income at the rate of nearly 15% a year from 1992 to 1997.

It has been said that generals win their battles by recruiting people, but corporate CEOs win theirs by firing them. At no time has this been as true as during the last two decades. In an article entitled The *Coming Collision*, Jesse Jackson quoted Marc Bayard of United For A Fair Economy as saying that in 1997, sixteen corporations had laid off 3,000 or more workers and that 13 of them gave their chief executive officers increased salaries, bonuses and stock options.

American Express, for example, announced layoffs of 3,300 workers in 1997 even as its profits increased dramatically. Its

CEO, Harvey Golub, earned an incredible 224 percent increase in take-home pay. His annual compensation of $33.4 million equaled the total annual pay of 1,500 employees earning the average U.S. 1997 weekly wage.

International Paper rewarded its CEO, John Dillon, a 140 percent increase in salary and bonuses in return for announced plans to lay off 10 percent of its work force of 9,125 workers.

Whirlpool Corporation gave its CEO a 47 percent pay hike plus more stock options after it announced 4,700 layoffs. Overall, writes Business Week, in 1997, the average CEO earned about 326 times the income of the average factory worker, up from 209 times the income of the average factory worker in 1996.[9]

The average CEOs did even better. In 1977, whereas they made 144 times the income of the average non-supervisory worker, in 1997 they made 273 times as much!

But to capture how inequality in wealth increased in just five years between 1992 and 1997, consider a Census Bureau stating that in 1992, the richest one percent of households owned 38 percent of all common stocks. By 1997, they owned 42 percent. In 1992, the bottom 90 percent of households owned only 19 percent of all common stocks, but by 1997 that 19 percent had dropped to 16 percent.[10]

Who now remembers the high-tech revolution in information technology, heralded with great fanfare that was supposed to create millions of well-paying jobs? "And yet," writes Robert Reich, Labor Secretary in the first Clinton administration, "almost all the gain from that 'revolution' has been going to people at the top." Citing figures released by the Congressional Budget Office, Reich noted that in the year 2000, those Americans with incomes in the top 2.7 million would have as many after-tax dollars to spend as those in the bottom 100 million altogether. The poorest one fifth of households would have an average income of $8,800, down from $10,000 in 1997. Since the start of the Clinton administration, the incomes of the richest one-fifth of American households have risen twice as fast as those in the middle fifth. And, adds Reich, "this calculation doesn't even include income from other perks such as stock options which have gone mostly to people at the top. And notably it does not include increases in the values of the rapidly growing stock portfolios. Add these into the mix and the wealth gap turns into the Grand Canyon."[11] In 1999, writes Holly Sklar, America had 268 billionaires. In just one year, in 2000, America added another 30 billionaires, making a total of 298 billionaires.[12] Today writes Molly Lazarotta of United for a Fair Economy, the financial wealth of the top one percent of households exceeds the combined wealth of the bottom 95 percent.[13]

By August 2001, the growing wealth inequality elicited the following comment by syndicated columnist Molly Ivins. Speaking of the tax cuts pushed through by the George W. Bush administration, which gave 42 percent of the cut to the wealthiest one percent of the citizens, she wrote that such a tax cut "is in fact class warfare. One cannot even make the pathetic argument that since the rich pay more in taxes, they should get a bigger cut. The top one percent pay only 21 percent of all federal taxes, but will get 43 percent of the tax cut, which if you do the math, is more than twice their share."

"I am so sorry," wrote Ivins, "that [treasury secretary] O'Neill is upset by people who refer to the corporate aristocracy as 'robber barons'. That is rude, isn't it? Personally I prefer to call them greedy bastards and to point out that there is absolutely no limit to their insatiable greed. The 1990 average CEO pay was 80 times that of the average worker; by 1999, it was 485 times that of the average worker.

"President Bush holds a press conference with his 'tax families' to show that a $25,000 a year waitress with two kids is a beneficiary of his tax cut, but according to the Center on Budget and Policy Priorities, under the Bush plan, 12 million lower end and moderate income families supporting 24 million children get absolutely nothing out of this tax cut.

This tax cut is beautifully designed and crafted to redistribute wealth from the poor to the rich".[14]

What Are the Causes of the Rising Inequality of Wealth in America?

The root cause of wealth inequality lies in the almost overwhelming power that business groups hold over the rest of the population, and above all, over the lives of working people. Business interests accumulate their wealth from the profits they have made in the past, and continue to make, from the labor of their employees.

Business also profits from the sale of goods and services, many of which are overpriced and that are bought by consumers, the vast majority of whom are working people.

Business uses part of its accumulated wealth to finance the election campaigns of many pro-business candidates in both major parties to make sure that Congress passes laws that benefit business interests. These laws include all kinds of tax cuts and loopholes, massive corporate subsidies, frequent and generous depreciation allowances and, most important of all, fat military contracts, all of which have been benefiting mainly the narrow interests of business over those of the vast majority of the population.

Business has also been using its wealth to buy up and concentrate ownership of all of the main television stations and almost all of the more important radio and print media to make sure that only views favorable to business interests are presented to the public. One lesson that the business class and in particular the large corporations have learned is that controlling the minds of the vast majority of working people is far easier and much less messy than controlling workers by means of physical coercion. They do this by filling the minds of working people with news about fires, crimes, celebrities, sports, and sex-infused drama. News of the blood and gore of the dead and wounded in the aftermath of the war on Iraq and its occupation is carefully hidden from view. Only very rarely are the interests and views of working people presented in any of the media, and one does not need to be very alert to notice that fact.

In his book, *The Politics of Rich and Poor*, Kevin Phillips pointed to two major causes for the widening wealth gap. One cause was the tax policies of the Reagan and the senior Bush administrations, and the other was the shift in spending from social needs to the military.

Phillips noted that while military spending rose from 23 percent of the federal budget in 1980 to 28 percent in 1987, spending for human resources dropped from 28 percent to 22 percent during the same period. This preference for defense over domestic priorities wreaked havoc on low-income families, especially those of the working poor, while it enriched the already very wealthy 10 percent who profited both directly and indirectly from defense contracts.

Rising military expenditures come from money borrowed by the Treasury Department. During the Reagan and the two Bush administrations, the Treasury Department had to borrow money for defense spending and this they did at a time when corporate and high income tax rates especially for the wealthy were drastically cut. Both the massive military expenditures and the huge tax cuts put the Federal government in debt. The Federal debt, for which the government had to pay interest, then grew by leaps and bounds. Interest on the borrowed money in the 1988 budget came to $218 billion. Of this sum, 80 percent was paid to families with incomes in the top 20 percent, at the very time when their tax rate dropped to 29 percent.

Phillips also noted that in 1952, corporations paid 32.1 percent of the total income taxes. By 1983, that figure had plummeted to 6.3 percent. Meanwhile, state and local taxes were increased, affecting disproportionately those least able to pay. From 1977 to 1988, while the income of the top one percent of families increased by 49.8 percent, their federal tax rate dropped from 30.9 percent in 1977 and to 23.1 percent in 1984.[15]

The tax cuts of the George W. Bush administration further widened the chasm of wealth inequality. As already noted, "The tax law of 2001 gave 42.5 percent of the cut to the wealthiest one percent, and to the 12 million lower and moderate income families with 24 million children, it gave absolutely nothing. Furthermore, 74 percent of taxpayers pay more in payroll taxes such as social security, Medicare, etc. than they do in income taxes. [According to this Bush tax law], a $26,000-a-year couple with two kids would ...[be] saving exactly $20, but they would still be paying $2,689 in payroll taxes... A middle-management couple with two kids making $180,000 a year would get a $2,000 tax break, but the $18,000 a year worker with wife and two kids would get nothing. This is unfair, unjust and wrong. It is class warfare waged by the robber baron rich against everybody else."[16]

The Increasing Rate of Exploitation of the Labor of Working People

Another very important factor contributing to the rising inequality and of great concern to numerous working families is the rate of exploitation of American workers. According to the 1987 Census of Manufacturers, the rate of exploitation of the labor of U.S. workers increased from about 100 percent in 1860 to close to 150 percent in 1950. By 1965 that rate surpassed 200 percent. By 1981 it reached 275 percent and by 1987 with the Reagan-led attack against unions, it reached the unprecedented level of 341 percent. The share of created value for production workers was reduced to only 22.7 percent. In other words, nearly 80 percent of the value of the products and services produced by workers went into the pockets of the owners of businesses, whereas only a little over 20 percent was paid as wages to workers. Such a magnitude of exploitation creates a yawning abyss between the wealth of the business owners and the workers. The Chamber of Commerce, which represents small and medium sized businesses, regularly boasts that the rate of profit accruing to employers is four to five times the average cost of wages.[17]

Another appalling cause of the rising wealth gap is the debt trap into which many American working class families have fallen and continue to fall more deeply with each passing year. Debt as a percentage of personal income rose from 58 percent in 1973 to 76 percent in 1989 to an estimated 85 percent in 1997.[18] By July 2001, the combined debt of all U.S. households had reached an incredible 106 percent of their total after tax income and is continuing to grow at an alarming rate. "Consumer debt has been rising rapidly and now accounts for about 22 percent of the after tax income" and that rise "is dwarfed by the increase in mortgage debt – mostly debt owed for owner occupied housing."[19]

Two factors cause the increase in mortgage debt: more aggressive borrowing with little or no down payment or borrowing against equity to finance other purchases. "The result is that homeowner equity has fallen dramatically. It equaled 83 percent of the value of their real estate in 1950, less than 70 percent in 1980 and only 54 percent at the end of 2000. As a result, families spend more than 14 percent of their after tax income on debt service, that is, one out of every seven dollars. That is more than the average household spends on food."[20]

"The consumer debt load for the average family has tripled in just one generation," writes Bob Herbert in the New York Times of November 10, 2003. "More and more Americans are using credit cards and other forms of borrowing to bridge the difficult gap between household income and the cost of essential goods and services. And those families, already in trouble, are ruthlessly exploited by a wide range of lenders.

"Struggling families that fall behind in their payments," continues Bob Herbert, "are like a gold mine to the credit card companies." According to the public policy group Demos, "late fees have become the fastest growing source of revenue for the [credit card] industry, jumping from $1.7 billion in 1996 to $7.3 billion in 2002. "With so many families living on the edge of a financial cliff, it's inevitable that a lot of them will fall off. Personal bankruptcies reached an all-time high of six million last year."[21]

UE News Service

" In recognition of your pension coming due
we are giving you your dismissal notice now..."

Other factors have also contributed to rising wealth inequality. Among them is the minimum wage that over the years has been reduced to a poverty wage. In 1979, adjusted for inflation, it was worth $6.39. By 1998, again adjusted for inflation, it was worth $5.15. The previous minimum wages allowed a full time worker with a wife and one child to bring his family above the official poverty line. The most recent minimum does not. That minimum has been stuck at $5.15 an hour since 1997 and is nearly 40 percent less in real terms compared to 1968. To match the 1968 level, today's minimum wage would be $8.45.

"At the current rate," writes Holly Sklar, "a single parent with one child would have to work more that two full time minimum wage jobs, while a couple with two children would have to work more than three full time minimum wage jobs to make ends meet."[22] Nathan Newman, a lawyer and community activist, writes that "conservative critics have always been against raising the minimum claiming that it increases unemployment, yet unemployment is higher today than back in 1968 when no one made less than $8 an hour.[23] According to a survey conducted by the Institute for Policy Studies and United for a Fair Economy, if the present minimum wage would be raised as high as the pay hikes of corporate executives, it would amount to $25.50.[24]

The erosion of pensions, decreasing access to affordable housing, the diminished ability to save, rising bankruptcies and vanishing family farms are some of the other factors that cause increasing wealth disparities.[25]

One of the most blatant causes of the wealth gap is in the billions of our tax dollars given as handouts by the Federal government to private corporations. A surprising exposure of such welfare handouts to corporations was published in a series of articles by Time Magazine. "During one of the most robust periods on our nation's history," write the authors of the articles, "the Federal government has shelled out $125 billion in corporate welfare, equivalent to all the income tax paid by 60 million individuals and families. Indeed thus far in the 1990s, corporate profits have totaled $4.5 billion – a sum equal to the paychecks of 50 million working Americans who earned less than $25,000 a year for eight years. Companies get government money to advertise their products, to help build new plants, offices and stores; and to train their workers. They [the companies] sell their goods to foreign buyers that make the acquisitions with tax dollars supplied by the U.S. government; engage in foreign transactions that are insured by the government; and are excused from paying a portion of their income tax if they sell products overseas. They pocket lucrative government contracts to carry out ordinary business operations and government grants to conduct research that will improve their profit margins. They are extended partial tax immunity if they locate in certain geographical areas, and they may write off as business expenses some of the perks enjoyed by their top executives.

"The justification for much of this welfare is that the U.S. government is creating jobs. Over the past six years, Congress appropriated $5 billion to run the Export-Import Bank of the United States, which subsidizes companies that sell goods abroad. James A. Harmon, president and chairman, puts it this way: "American workers...have higher quality, better-paying jobs, thanks to Eximp bank's financing." But the numbers at the bank's five biggest beneficiaries – AT&T, Bechtel, Boeing, General Electric and McDonnell Douglas (now a part of Boeing) – tell another story. At these companies, which have accounted for about 40% of all loans, grants and long-term guarantees in this decade, overall employment has fallen 38%, as more than a third of a million jobs have disappeared. The picture is much the same at the state and local level, where a different kind of feeding frenzy is taking place. Politicians stumble over one another in the rush to arrange special deals for select corporations, fueling a growing economic war among the states. The result is that states keep throwing money at companies that in many cases are not serious about moving anyway. The companies are certainly not reluctant to take the money, though, which is available if they simply utter the word 'relocation.' And why not?

Corporate executives, after all, have a fiduciary duty to squeeze every dollar they can from every locality waving blandishments in their face. State and local governments now give corporations money to move from one city to another, even from one building to another, and tax credits for hiring new employees. They supply funds to train workers or pay part of their wages while they are in training, and provide scientific and engineering assistance to solve workplace technical problems. They repave existing roads and build new ones. They lend money at bargain-basement interest rates to erect plants or buy equipment. They excuse corporations from paying sales and property taxes and relieve them from taxes on investment income."[26]

Louis Uchitelle of the New York Times reports that "there is no official data on how much is distributed in subsidies across the country. Alan Peters, a professor of urban planning at the University of Iowa, and one or two other academics have tried to estimate the total loss of city and state tax revenue through abatements, lower income taxes, outright payments, training grants, wage subsidies and the like [to corporations]. Their estimates start at $30 billion a year and range up to $50 billion, with Peters putting the number at somewhere in the $40 billions, based on recent tax expenditures. Mr. Uchitelle quotes Mr. Peters as saying that 'It seems like almost every state is giving away grandmother, grandfather, the family jewels, you name it, everything.' One way or another, the cities and states, in forfeiting more than $30 billion in tax revenue, are channeling to the private sector, enough [money] to hire 375,000 school teachers at $50,000 a year, plus benefits.[27]

Donald Barlett and James Steele laid out a detailed expose of corporate welfare. They wrote that the Fortune 500 companies have erased more jobs than they have created this past decade [of the 1990s] and yet, they are the biggest beneficiaries of corporate welfare. If corporate welfare is an unproductive end game, why does it keep growing in a period of intensive government cost cutting? For starters, it has good public relations and an army of bureaucrats working to expand it. A corporate-welfare bureaucracy of an estimated 11,000 organizations and agencies has grown up with access to city halls, state houses, the Capitol and the White House. They conduct seminars, conferences, and training sessions. They have their own trade associations. They publish their own journals and newsletters. They create attractive web sites on the Internet. And they never call it 'welfare.' They call it 'economic incentives' or 'empowerment zones' or 'enterprise zones'."[28]

In another article, Barlett and Steele report that, "Just about every large U.S. corporation – Intel, Eastman Kodak, General Motors, Caterpillar, Union Carbide, Chrysler, R .J. Reynolds and Georgia Pacific, to name just a few corporations, have opened offices in the U.S. Virgin Islands, Jamaica and Barbados, and in twenty-nine other countries, [and] pay no federal income taxes on a portion of their export profits, and it is all legal. Such corporations can shelter fifteen percent or more of their export earnings."[29]

Some wit once quipped that what we have in America is socialism for the rich and capitalism for the poor. In other words, working people are set up to compete for jobs in a job market that is deliberately engineered to produce a scarcity of jobs, while many businesses, mostly giant corporations, are provided huge supports by the federal, state and local governments, relieving **them** of the need to compete for survival.

How Rising Income Inequality Increases Mass Unemployment

To get a better idea of why great wealth disparity creates large numbers of unemployed workers, it is helpful to compare the decade of the 1990s to the decade of the 1920s. The political economies of both decades were strikingly similar in that both were marked by great inequality in income and wealth.

Both decades produced new advanced technologies that radically transformed the production process. At the turn of the century, electric machines began to replace the steam engine. In 1914 just 30 percent of the energy-consuming machines with a total of nine million horsepower were run by electric power. By 1929, 70 percent of those machines with a total of 35 million horsepower were operated by electricity. Another technological breakthrough was the assembly line. By dividing the work process and imposing a uniform speed upon all workers, the assembly line brought about an amazing increase in productivity. This means that fewer workers have been able to produce many more goods. For example, prior to assembly line production, it took one worker 25 minutes to assemble a magnetic fly wheel; with an assembly line conveyor belt, that operation took 5 minutes, a 5-fold increase in productivity.[30] During the 1990s, the computer and its related technologies produced similar radical transformations in productivity.[31] The crucial factor in both decades was the enormous increase in productivity per worker alongside rising inequality in wealth and income between the richest fifth and the rest of the population. By 1929, though the real income of labor grew, the same number of workers in manufacturing produced one and a half times more production than the previous decade.[32] Similarly, during the 1990s, American factories were producing five times as much as they did in 1946 but with the same 12.3 million workers. Both periods also had similar official unemployment rates. During the 1920s, the official unemployment rate was at least 4 percent for seven of those years. For the 1990s that rate was an average of about 5.5 percent. This is more than 30% higher. And in both decades, the official unemployment rate took no account of the widespread part time and underemployed workers.[33]

Another feature similar to both decades was the sharp inequality of income and wealth. During the 1920s, 20% of the population collected over half of the total personal income, while 42 percent of households lived at or below a subsistence-to-poverty level and another 36 percent were at a 'minimum comfort' level. During the 1990s, the top one percent held 40 percent of the nation's household wealth.[34] By the year 2000, the richest 2.7 million Americans, comprising the top one percent of the population, will have as many after tax dollars to spend as the bottom 100 million together.[35]

To sum up, in both the 1920s and the 1990s, the wealthy had accumulated so much of the nation's wealth and the working people had so little of it that the latter were not able to buy enough of the goods and services that were available. The unsold goods and services cut deeply into the profits of both large and small corporations, which then began laying off millions of workers. By 1934, one out of every four workers or 25 percent of the workforce was out of work. The wealthy who had accumulated great wealth by virtue of their ownership of the means of production and distribution could consume only part of that wealth. But with the markets flooded with unsold goods, thus dimming the outlook for profits, businesses saw no reason to make any further investments, and in fact, laid off millions of workers and even cut the wages of those they retained.

Unemployment with its attendant miseries for millions of workers lasted ten years and was alleviated only partially by the limited spending of the Roosevelt administration. By 1938, about 17 million workers were still without jobs. The Great Depression came to an end only with the enormous government expenditures for the weapons and other equipment for the Second World War.

A similar process occurred during the recession of the years 2000 and 2001. Then also the 1990s saw a great surge in advanced technology. Companies began investing in factories to produce computers, software, cell-phones and a variety of other high tech goods, and the dot-com startups provided a small fraction of the population with great wealth. Companies were also introducing more advanced technology into their production processes to replace entire armies of middle managers and other types of employees.[36]

However, as during the Great Depression, most working people were not paid enough to be able to buy most of the goods and services that were produced.

Faced with vast piles of unsold goods and services, the corporations laid off hundreds of thousands of workers. From October 2000 to December 2001, in addition to the millions that were previously unemployed, some 2.6 million working people also lost their jobs. That translates into the overall official unemployment rate of 5.7 percent. Professor Lynch of Tufts University predicted an even higher unemployment rate of as high as 7 percent.[37] This means that 9-10 million working people would be without jobs and this, it needs to be kept in mind, is the official count which is much less than the real number of jobless.

Chapter Eight

Business's Unending Introduction and Use of Advanced Technology as a Cause of Mass Unemployment

In just about every sector of the economy, new technology has been displacing and will continue to displace millions of workers, especially those who are relatively well-paid but many others as well.

Between 1945 and 1955, the over 43,000 strikes that occurred were so damaging to the interests of business that the advent of technology to replace humans has been nothing less than utopia for the business community. Examples abound.

In its plant in Orion, Michigan, with 138 welding robots and 10 painting robots, General Motors turns out 270,000 cars per year, using 5,500 workers working two shifts, five days a week. Without the new technology, it would take 3,000 more employees to put out the same number of cars.[1]

The use of robots solves several other problems for the corporations. Robots increase reliability of production by minimizing disruption due to human error. Most importantly, by greatly reducing the number of workers employed, automation produces impressive gains in output per worker.[2] In 1948, it took 713,000 American and Canadian workers to produce 6 million vehicles. Thirty years later, nearly the same number of workers produced 13.2 million vehicles.[3] This increase in productivity provides a very impressive increase in corporate profits.

Advanced technology laid off thousands of steel workers. Whereas in 1980, United States Steel, the largest American steel company, employed 120,000 workers, by 1990, it produced about the same volume of steel by using just 20,000 workers. The future for steel workers loomed even bleaker as even more advanced devices were being planned for use in the manufacturing process.[4] In 1945, the Ford-owned Rouge plant housed 85,000 workers. Just 15 years later, the employment rolls plummeted to less than 30,000.[5] Between 1965 and 1995, machinists underwent a fate similar to the steel workers. During that period, 400,000 machinists lost their jobs.[6] In manufacturing operations across the entire Northern and Western industrial belt, the forces of automation continued to take their toll on unskilled African-American workers, leaving tens of thousands of permanently unemployed men and women in their wake.[7] In the 1960s, in the nation's largest cities, New York, Chicago, Philadelphia, and Detroit, where Blacks made up a large percentage of the unskilled blue collar work force, more than a million manufacturing, wholesale, and retail jobs were lost, many the result of technology displacement.[8] In the tire industry, Goodyear produced 30% more tires in 1992 than in 1988 and did it with 24,000 fewer employees.[9]

In the mining industries, in 1992, 45,000 jobs were eliminated.[10] In the chemical industry, productivity soared between 1959 and 1964. But the workers declined from 112,500 to 81,900 due to digital computer control.[11] In the electronics industry, General Electric reduced its worldwide employment from 400,000 in 1981 to less than 230,000 in 1993 while tripling its sales, all due to the introduction of new highly automated equipment on the factory floor.[12] In the household appliance industry, between 1973 and 1991, employment declined sharply from 196,300 to 117,100. And the Bureau of Labor Statistics predicts that by the year 2005, a mere 93,500 workers will be producing the nation's total output of home appliances.[13] In the service industries, new information technologies have raised productivity and displaced workers in all the service-related industries. AT&T, for instance, replaced more than 6,000 long distance operators with computerized voice-recognition technology. The company also cut 400 management jobs.[14]

Between 1983 and 1993, banks eliminated 179,000 human tellers, replacing them with automated teller machines. By the year 2000, more than 90% of banking customers will use automated teller machines.[15] A human teller can complete up to 200 transactions a day, working approximately 30 hours a week; he or she also gets sick leave, vacation and other benefits, all of which add up to significant costs to the banks. An ATM can handle 2,000 transactions a day, work 168 hours a week and requires no sick leave, vacation or benefits.[16] Thus have ATMs eliminated many battalions of tellers.

In the insurance industry, Mutual Benefit Life and Aetna Life and Casualty Company have both reduced their workforce. MBL eliminated 100 field office staff while Aetna reduced its staff to 2,300. By 1995, Aetna cut 5,000 employees, or 9% of its workforce.[17] New electronic office equipment is changing the way offices now work. Between 1983 and 1993, the nation's secretarial pool shrank by 8% to about 3.6 million.[18] The same thing has been happening to receptionists. They are being reduced in number and in some firms, eliminated all together.[19]

Two or three decades ago, when you called a business, you heard a real human voice. It was a receptionist, who responded to your call within a minute or two. Now, new technology provides an infinite number of menus from which to choose, and when we finally hear a real human voice, we breathe a sigh of relief. But for businesses in general, the new menu technology eliminates an army of receptionists. No longer is it necessary to pay their wages and benefits, thus swelling profits. In the wholesale and retail sectors, some 60,000 jobs were lost in 1992. Since 1989, the wholesale sector has lost more than a quarter million jobs.[20] Sears eliminated a staggering 50,000 jobs from its merchandising division in 1993, while its sales revenues rose by more than 10%.[21]

Drive-thru restaurants have become so highly automated that 6-8 employees can serve as many customers at peak hours of operation as 20 employees working in a sit-down fast food restaurant.[22] Home TV shopping has eliminated 411,000 retail jobs since 1989.[23] In a wide-ranging article, Simon Head tells us how advanced technology has been introduced into the service industries. "Re-engineering," as it is called, became common in the 1990s when computer software became increasingly capable of doing the job of large numbers of workers in hundreds of companies. One case of re-engineering cited by Head epitomizes how it works.

The IBM Credit Corporation, a subsidiary of IBM, provides credit for clients wishing to purchase IBM products. Several years ago, specialists were responsible for each stage of the business. The low level managers and skilled clerical workers in one department logged in credit applications. Another department's employees inserted special conditions for particular clients. In a third department, employees fixed the appropriate rate of interest, and yet another department gathered all the relevant information into a 'quote letter' to be sent to the IBM salesman and his customer. The entire system depended on large quantities of paperwork creeping slowly from one specialist's department to another. Re-engineering teams descended upon these clerical assembly lines and swept them away. In their place they installed software that, in all but a few exceptional cases, allows a single employee called a "deal structurer" to accomplish the functions once divided among many workers in various departments. The productivity of IBM's credit business increased not by 100 percent but by 10,000 percent.[24]

Here are some more examples from other industries:

- Apple Computer designed a new assembly plant in which just 100 persons aided by another 100 support staff and assisted by robots produces 72,000 Macintoshes in just 100 days.[25]
- General Electric calculated that on a two-shift basis over a five-year period, robots can perform at an average cost of $4 an hour. That is a mere third of the human cost.[26]
- Caterpillar Corporation invested $600 million in a high tech plant that eliminated 20,000 jobs.[27]
- Conventional seafaring vessels used to be loaded and unloaded by up to 150 longshoremen, but by 1980, the same work on the largest container ship using the most advanced technology was done by fewer than 30 men.[28]

By 1992, American factories were producing five times as much as they did in 1946. Yet the 12.3 million workers on the assembly lines in 1945 remained virtually unchanged in 1972.[29]

Why are corporations constantly introducing more advanced technologies into their plants and services? To understand why, we must first assume a general truth, which is that businessmen, whether small, medium or large, own businesses not to provide jobs and services to people who need them but to make a profit, preferably a large profit. There are surely other motives: for instance, the satisfaction of providing useful products and services. However, such motives cannot compete with the desire for profits, because no business can survive without profits. And because wages and salaries are more often a substantial part of operating costs – costs that often cut deeply into their profits – businesses are always seeking ways to reduce those costs. One major way businesses reduce costs is by introducing advanced technology. A single piece of advanced technology will generally do far more work at less cost than many employees, and thus will reduce or completely eliminate the need for those employees.

Will there ever be an end to the displacement of masses of both well-paid and poorly paid workers in the heavy industries and the services? When President Clinton, in 1992, expressed concern to a group of economists about creating more factory jobs, Professor Krugman of the Massachusetts Institute of Technology held out little hope. He said that, "The long term trend in manufacturing is recapitulating the long term trend in farming. During the past century we've had rapid productivity growth in farming and the result is fewer farmers."[30]

So what Professor Krugman was saying is that the same processes that occurred in the industrial and service sectors have taken place in the country's farms. In the same way that the Federal government subsidized and provided general support to big business in the urban areas, it has done the same to the country's farms. That is to say, it has given overwhelmingly greater support to big farms with consequences catastrophic to family farms.

The federal government has given the top 10% of American farmers 71% of subsidy money or 80.5 billion dollars of the total 114 billion dollars given to all the country's farmers.[31]

New technology, such as new breeding techniques, new kinds of seeds, more efficient fertilizers, pesticides, and other chemicals have become too expensive for family farmers. Family farmers in hundreds of counties in the rural plains of the Midwest have been compelled to abandon farming because of the inability to compete with the large agribusinesses and factory-style farmers.[32]

According to Willard Cochrane, professor emeritus at the University of Minnesota, "the total number of farms in United States has declined from 6.5 million in 1935 to 2.05 million in 1997, with most of the decline among family farms. More than 60% of the remaining farms are resource, residential, or retirement farms.

As a consequence of the new technology, many rural areas are being drained of their young. "From the Dakotas to the Texas Panhandle, the rural Great Plains have been losing people for 70 years, a slow demographic collapse."[33]

"Some of the rural counties in the Midwest lost 40% of their 18-25 year olds to semi-urban and urban centers...Most everywhere, about one sixth of the land mass in the United States, populations are at modern lows.

"You don't have young people taking over the farms, and you don't have businesses staying. Even the parents are telling their kids to get out. There is very little to keep many of these [rural] towns going," said Mr. Jon Bailey of the center for rural affairs."[34]

In 1944, a mechanical cotton picker picked a thousand pounds of cotton in one hour, a job that was previously done by

50 persons at the same length of time. By 1972, cotton-picking machines displaced every single human cotton picker. Because cotton was picked by their share-cropping tenants, the plantation owners evicted millions of them, leaving them homeless and jobless.

Between 1940 and 1970, more than 5 million African-Americans, men, women, and children, migrated North in search of work. But about the same time that the South was introducing the new cotton picker, the North was introducing automatic machinery in the manufacturing industries. Between 1953 and 1962, for instance, 1.6 million blue collar unskilled workers, tens of thousands of them African-Americans, were displaced by those new machines.[35]

As long as the dominant motive of business continues to be the unending pursuit of profits at the expense of jobs, more and more advanced technology will likely be introduced, and an unending number of jobs will disappear.

Chapter Nine

The Export of Jobs as a Major Cause of Mass Unemployment

"When I jumped into the labor movement in the late 1970s, our manufacturing unions were being hit hard as corporations pursued the 'runaway' strategy. Companies were downsizing or closing their northern and mid-western factories and scooping up taxpayer-financed corporate welfare to reopen primarily in the U.S. south and southwest.

What began as a corporate and government strategy to reduce wages and increase profits by moving to southern states has now become a tidal wave of job migration out of the country entirely. The 'runaway' problem is now called 'globalization.' We are literally witnessing the dismantling of one of the most productive and diverse manufacturing economies in human history...

The hard numbers of this job exodus are shocking: more than 10,000 U.S. manufacturing facilities have shut down just since 1993 and more every day."

Chris Townsend, Labor Party Press, July 2001

Among the factors that have been contributing to mass unemployment is the export of millions of jobs by American corporations.

This chapter will tell about the number of American jobs that have been lost through the export of capital and factories by American corporations during the last three or four decades.

We will describe the kinds of jobs that have been lost, where the jobs have been going, why the corporations are taking their capital to other countries, the role of the Federal government in promoting the export of jobs and finally the consequences of U.S. job losses for America's working people.

How Many and What Kind of Jobs Are Being Lost

No government agency has ever kept records about the number of U.S. jobs that have been lost as a consequence of the flood of capital and factories sent out of the country by the transnational corporations (TNCs) and other American corporations. Whatever information exists about job losses is scattered in various U.S. newspapers and periodicals and some progressive institutions. What follows are several of those reports.

The shrinking of U.S. jobs began in the 1980s with the transfer overseas of about a million or more jobs in the apparel industry. Such jobs have been shifted to almost every country in Asia and Latin America. For instance, by 1997, 25,000 young Vietnamese workers were churning out one million pairs of Nikes every month. At that time, Vietnam's minimum wage was $42.00 per month. Americans paid $149.50 for a pair of Nike basketball shoes, for which Vietnamese workers were paid $1.50.[1] Figure out, dear reader, the profit Nike makes every month from the manufacture of 1 million pairs of shoes.

American apparel companies, such as J.C. Penney, Sears, Wal-Mart and Montgomery Ward, contract with Asian companies to hire workers in Nicaragua, a country of very high unemployment. Paid according to a piece rate, [that is a wage for every individual garment they sew], workers receive $3.00-$5.00 a day, and during peak manufacturing periods, as much as $10.00 a day. To get an idea of the scale of profits made from the labor of tens of thousands of employees, the vast majority of them women, one of the workers reported she was paid $1.35 for every one hundred pairs of jeans pockets she attached. The minimum wage in Nicaragua is 41 cents an hour, but other tremendous incentives for foreign investors are total exemption on income taxes for the first ten years of operation, exemption on sales and capital gains tax, and on the import of raw materials and machinery, no duties on exports, and no quotas on textile imports, and low rental costs for industrial space.[2]

In El Salvador, employees sewing Kathie Lee shirts earn the equivalent of $4.79 a day, which covers only one third of the cost of living in that country. Employees were screamed at, the factories were very hot, the bathrooms were dirty, and the employees were not allowed to look from one side to the other nor to get up to drink water. As a consequence, all of the employees developed kidney trouble and headaches from the heat.[3]

Far worse are the working conditions of employees in Sri Lanka. They produce toys for Disney under abusive and violent conditions, while being paid 16 cents per hour, earning $11.27 for a seventy hour week.[4]

Unimaginably abysmal are the conditions of workers in Bangladesh. They sew shirts and pants for Wal-Mart and other retailers. At one factory, about a thousand workers, 80% of them young women, are forced to work from 7:30 a.m. to 8:00 p.m. seven days a week, and are paid just nine to twenty cents an hour, with no health care or maternity leave, screamed at to work faster, with monitored bathroom visits and fired for daring to complain or ask for their rights. There are 3,500 garment factories in Bangladesh employing 1.6 million garment workers, and not a single union with a contract. So low are the wages paid to the workers that it amounts to less than one tenth of one percent of the retail price of the caps that they produce, which is $17.43. All of the costs, such as labor, shipping, and the factory owner's profits, add up to $1.23. That means that the retailer in the U.S. makes a profit of 1,300%.

American companies and their contractors in Bangladesh pay no corporate, property, local or state taxes, no income tax, not even a sales tax, and no import or export duties. U.S. companies imported 924 million garments made in Bangladesh, with a wholesale customs value of over 2.2 billion dollars.[5]

A startling fact about all of this apparel work being done offshore is that American workers have lost 1.3 million manufacturing jobs in the apparel industry just in 2001.[6]

Corporations like Wal-Mart, J.C. Penney, Target and Sears contract apparel work in American Samoa. There, workers toil under conditions of indentured servants described as a "nightmare." Until it was closed in January 2001, a Korean owned factory employed 251 Vietnamese so called "guest workers," more than 90% of them women. Some of the women were beaten, kicked and slapped, were watched by the factory bosses while they showered or dressed, were fed a thin, watery gruel of rice and cabbage, thus reducing some of the workers to walking skeletons. They slept two women in a bunk bed 36 inches wide, in barracks infested with rats eating through the women's clothes, with feces backed up through the shower drains, and with no soap or toilet paper in the bathrooms. Instead of the $2.60 minimum wage law in Samoa, some workers were paid as little as $1.22 an hour and were, even so, paid only intermittently.[7]

China is the Garden of Eden for corporations seeking cheap labor. Disney, for instance, makes well over 90% of its toys in China. They are made by young women who are forced to work from 7:00 a.m. to 10:00 p.m. and earn just 18 cents an hour. By the time they reach 25 years of age, they are fired because they are 'used up' and may get pregnant. The factory will not pay maternity benefits.[8]

Can one imagine Americans being charged anywhere near 16 cents for those toys?

From 1980 to 1995, the U. S. lost more than 500,000 textile and apparel jobs.[9] In 1992 Jack Sheinkman, President of the Amalgamated Clothing and Textile Workers Union, reported that 2 to 6 million manufacturing jobs had been lost due to the Reagan and Bush administrations active efforts to persuade American businesses to move abroad. This has devastated America's textile and apparel industries.[10]

The Export of Well-Paid Industrial Jobs

The 1970s saw the beginning of a massive outflow of well paid industrial jobs. At first, most of these were jobs in the auto and steel industry, but in time, it included every kind of well-paid, highly skilled jobs. A grim and illuminating tale of job losses was told to a Congressional Committee on January 18, 1980 by Ronald Delia, president of Local 923 of the United Auto Workers. He told of the shock and humiliation underwent by laid off workers and their communities. He told of Ford's continuous investments overseas – investments that have created hardships not only for the workers at Pico, but also for the U.S. economy. Ford, Chrysler and General Motors, he said, produce one third of their entire production overseas, and the amount of their imported cars sold in Southern California "capture an unbelievable 48 percent of the market here.."

Delia asked why is it that Ford does not modernize its Pico plant, which it could do with a limited amount of capital expenditure, instead of spending billions building plants overseas and forcing out of work its senior workers. He also accused the Big Three (auto companies) of stifling rapid transit and other forms of ground transportation just to reap large profits on large automobiles, without any concern to advance technology in energy saving automobiles, which produce smaller profits.[11]

While millions of Americans lost their jobs as a result of the recession engineered by the Reagan administration, Ford's fortunes did not even suffer as much as a dent. Just five months after Delia's statement to the Congressional Committee, the Wall Street Journal told its readers that Ford was enjoying a boom in its operations in Mexico, where it was planning to expand by building a $365 million plant to make cylinder engines.[12]

From 1967 to 1976, 1.5 million manufacturing jobs were lost in the northeastern and midwestern states. Those states were the strongholds of America's heavy industry, providing jobs that were relatively well paid because they were unionized.[13] In a three-year period from 1977-1980, nearly every U.S. corporation closed factories, many of them permanently. United States Steel Corporation laid off workers in Gary, Youngstown and Pittsburgh.[14]

Up to 1980, U.S. Steel alone discharged 13,000 steel workers.[15] From 1969 to 1976, New York City alone lost 620,000 industrial jobs.[16] Between 1969 and 1979, Akron, Ohio, long the center of the U.S. rubber industry, lost 16,000 of its 100,000 manufacturing jobs.[17]

By September 1980, reports William Serrin, about 340,00 blue- and white-collar workers in U.S. auto firms had been laid off or discharged. An estimated 1,000,000 workers in the automative supply industries had lost their jobs.[18]

By 1991, 500,000 jobs and 2,000 factories had been shifted to Mexico. Rudy Oswald, the AFL-CIO's chief economist, reported that between 1989-1991, the U.S. electronics industry alone lost 440,000 jobs and the auto industry lost 140,000 jobs.[19] Seymour Melman, professor of industrial engineering at Columbia University, wrote that from 1977 to 1987, fifty percent of production workers' jobs were lost to the machine industry, sixty percent to the farm machinery industry, forty three percent to the turbine and turbine generator industry, forty two percent to the construction machinery manufacturers, sixty percent to the mining equipment industry, 43 percent to the textile equipment industry and sixty eight percent to the oil and gas filled equipment industry.[20]

In 1977, the Department of Commerce found that 3,540 U.S. companies had 24,666 foreign affiliates. By 1980, foreign affiliates had a combined direct investment stake of about $200 billion compared to $12 billion in 1950.[21] For every billion dollars of foreign investment by U.S. industrial firms, about 26,500 U.S. jobs are eliminated. This means that the $200 billion invested abroad transferred about 5,300,000 jobs from the U.S. to the overseas operations of American corporations.

By 1970, in all industries, U.S. multinational corporations were employing 4,780,000 people outside the U.S. In the manufacturing industry, however, foreign employment by U.S. firms amounted to 3,293,000 people. The foreign affiliates of U.S. manufacturing firms produced two to three times as much as they exported from the U.S. In the automotive industry, American overseas firms exported 4.6 times what they produced in the U.S. American machine industry firms exported more than 1.5 times as much as they produced in the U.S.[22]

In their book, *Corporate Flight*, Bluestone, Harrison and Baker reported that in 1969 and 1976, as many as 15,000,000 well paid jobs were lost as a result of plant shutdowns by American corporations.[23] Those millions of job losses occurred even before the 1994 implementation of the North American Free Trade Act of the Americas (NAFTA). Since 1994, NAFTA has eliminated another 766,030 actual and potential jobs. Even that, says Robert Scott of the Economic Policy Institute, "is just the most visible tip of NAFTA's impact on the U.S. economy. NAFTA has also contributed to rising income inequalities, suppressed real wages for production workers, weakened their collective bargaining powers and their ability to organize unions and reduced fringe benefits."[24]

More will be said below on how job exports have affected American workers and whole communities.

Where Have the Jobs Been Going

The jobs that American working people are losing by the millions are being sent by U.S. corporations all over the world, where hundreds of millions of people are so destitute that they are willing to work for wages that are one tenth or less than the average American wage.

GM opened its first factory in Mexico in 1935 assembling trucks in the capital from parts sent from the U.S. Then encouraged by a 1965 Mexican law to produce goods for export tax free, GM built an entire parts industry there in the 1980s. Larry Mathews, a spokesman for Flint's United Auto Workers Local 651, said at that time that Flint's Delphi East factory originally had 13,000 workers; by 1998 it had fewer than 6,000 workers. Meanwhile, Ford Motor Corporation had built eleven parts factories in Mexico.

Sam Dillon reported that before NAFTA became law, the financial advantage of producing parts in Mexico was substantial, but that since NAFTA went into effect in 1994, those advantages have only increased.[25] But Mexico is hardly the only foreign country into which GM has poured billions of dollars.

Keith Bradsher reported that GM is building new assembly plants in Argentina, Brazil, Poland, Thailand and China.[26] Intel Corporation is a major employer in Malaysia. The U.S. steel industry, which was booming in 1995, yet was a third smaller that it had been in 1975, gradually has been moving to other countries.[27] Motorola built a new $750 million water fabrication plant in China and expected to have 12,000 Chinese employees by the year 2000.[28] While Motorola was enlisting the U.S. government to advance its global interests, the company's worldwide work force had by 1995 reached 142,000, but the U.S. share of the work force declined to 56 percent.[29]

China is fast becoming a major outlet for U.S. capital investments, which zoomed from $358 million in 1990, to $56 billion in just five years. From a few dozen firms actively lobbying on behalf of free trade with China, by 1997, that number had mushroomed to 800. Boeing shut down a plant in Kansas and opened one in Xian, China where workers are paid $50 a month.[30]

In 1985 General Electric Corporation had 243,000 employees in the U.S. By 1996, that number decreased to 155,000. During the same period GE increased its foreign employment from 56,000 to 84,000 workers.[31] So while millions of the jobs of American workers have gone to foreign countries, one estimate is that profits reaped by U.S. transnational corporations increased from $9 billion in 1969 to $42 billion in just ten years. From 1970 to 1980, U.S. income from foreign investment increased from $11 billion to $76 billion, a seven fold increase.[32] And that was long before the 1994 NAFTA pact which opened the floodgates to the export of jobs and to the super profits of the transnational corporations.

Our southern neighbor, Mexico, was by 1991 home to 2,000 factories, most of which were owned by U.S corporations.[33] Mexico now has over 3,000 mostly U.S. owned factories whose workers earn an average of $3.40 a day.[34] Many businesses have been lured to Mexico by consultants who advertise annual savings to U.S. corporations of between $16,000 to $26,000 per worker per year.

Dillon went on to report that since 1978, General Motors has built more the 50 parts factories in Mexico which by 1998 employed 72,000 workers. In one of those, Mexican workers earn $1 to $2 an hour producing instrument panels and steering wheels for GM cars and trucks. Those very same instruments were until just a few years ago produced by American workers at GM's Delphi East factory in Flint, Michigan and they were earning $22 an hour.

When NAFTA was pushed through Congress, President Clinton who promoted and signed it could not find enough words to praise it as an unqualified success. But as we have already noted above, Robert E. Scott of the Economic Policy Institute, a Washington based think tank, reported that by April 2001, NAFTA had eliminated 766,030 actual and potential U.S. jobs, contributed to rising income inequality, suppressed real wages for production workers, has weakened the collective bargaining power of working people and their ability to organize unions and has reduced fringe benefits.

Why Are the Corporations Exporting Jobs to Other Countries?

The Agency for International Development (AID), has spent billions of American taxpayer dollars to establish and promote offshore manufacturing, as the result of a dramatic shift in foreign policy under the Reagan administration. This policy, known as "Trade Not Aid," made the private sector, rather than foreign governments, the target of American foreign aid packages. The [declared] aim of this program was to encourage the growth of democratic, free-market economies around the globe. Not coincidentally, the degree of poverty in developing countries is so great that workers gratefully line up for jobs offering wages at a small percent of the American minimum wage. As a result, U.S. manufacturers with offshore production sites are at a distinct competitive advantage [over domestic manufacturers.] The lower the wages in a developing country, the lower the cost of production for a multinational company, and the greater the profits and competitive edge in producing low cost finished products.

From 1978 to 1991, 2.6 million manufacturing jobs were lost in the United States. Nearly a half million of those jobs were lost in the textile and apparel industries. In El Salvador, Guatemala and Honduras, the National Labor Committee found thirty U.S. apparel manufacturers operating their own plants there, and another 68 companies with subcontracting relationships. Meanwhile, over 12,000 American workers lost their jobs in the textile and apparel industries.[35]

An ad appearing in the August 1990 U.S. apparel trade journal, _Bobbin_, read, "Rosa Martinez produces apparel for U.S. markets on her sewing machine in El Salvador. You can hire her for 57 cents an hour." This ad was placed by an organization called FUSADES (Salvadoran Foundation for Economic and Social Development). This business development organization has received 94% of its budget, over $102 million, from the U.S. Aid for International Development. FUSADES' mission is to supply low-cost labor to American companies producing apparel, electronic and other labor-intensive products. "A manufacturing production worker in El Salvador earns about 40 cents an hour, or $3.20 a day or $915 a year. This wage level is less than one-twentieth the average manufacturing wage in the United States."[36]

In VietNam, the minimum wage is $42 per month. Writes Jeff Ballinger, director of Press for Change, "At that rate, labor for a pair of basketball shoes which retail for $149.50 costs Nike $1.50, 1 percent of the retail value." Vietnamese newspapers in America report that Nike workers in VietNam are subjected to numerous labor rights violations, including verbal, physical and sexual abuse and overtime work far in excess of permissible limits.[37]

It was the communications revolution that made it possible for corporations to move entire factories and other capital assets to foreign countries and to control from their headquarters in the U.S. their far-flung sweatshop operations. The chief economist of Dunn and Bradstreet Corporation explained that only recently have inexpensive telecommunications, computer management systems and cheap transportation made it possible for company managers to look upon the entire world as a grid on which they can search for the best manufacturing sites and the best marketing opportunities. What the chief economist meant by " best manufacturing sites" are those foreign lands where workers that are employed by U.S transnational corporations are not paid minimum wages, enjoy no benefits, are granted no sick leave or pensions, and are commonly forbidden to unionize or to strike. And given the extreme poverty of so many millions of them, they are happy to find work in sweatshop conditions, meaning abysmally low wages, long hours, oppressive physical conditions and harsh discipline.[38]

The primary motive driving this gigantic exodus of jobs is the corporation's insatiable drive for super-profits. But that is not the only motive. It is also the relentless drive for power that such super-profits make possible. It is the power to control the working conditions of unionized and non-unionized workers. It is the power to keep them weak and docile through the creation of mass unemployment. It is the power to control the various branches of government and to buy up as many of the media as possible, especially that of the television media, so as to control what is broadcast. This they do in order to try to trivialize, politically neutralize or dumb down the thinking of working people.

Many employers have never been happy with having to pay even the minimum wages required by law nor to increase it when needed due to inflation and the rising cost of living. They have opposed efforts to bring non-union workers into unions. Nor have they liked the fact that since 1935 working people no longer have had to be too fearful of being fired because they could, at least for a short time, rely on unemployment compensation to soften the blow of job loss.[39]

The Role of the Federal Government in the Export of Jobs

As incredible at it may sound, the federal government and its affiliated agencies have actually helped American transnational corporations to move U.S. jobs to foreign countries. And it has unashamedly used taxpayers money to do just that.

Businessmen in America have always had close relations with the Federal government. Those relationships go all the way back to pre-Civil War days, but they have become very cozy since the end of the Second World War.

At the end of that war, most western industrialized countries had substantial restrictions on the movement of capital across borders for conducting trade, to make investments or simply to hold foreign currencies. Such controls allowed progressive governments to fix appropriate interest rates, free of the fear that the wealthy would take their capital abroad if other countries paid higher rates. Lower rates would allow accelerated development of the economy and therefore would create more jobs. By the late 1970s, however, western governments began to remove those restrictions. By 1975 the U.S. had already removed most controls over capital.[40]

The export of goods and capital to a war-devastated Europe as part of the post-war Marshall Plan was the first step in the long march toward the expansion of American transnational corporations all over the world. And that first step, like the numerous others that came after it, was funded by the taxes paid to the Federal government mostly by working people. Starting in the seventies, the export of goods was soon dwarfed by the export of capital and jobs.[41]

The Commerce Department has been the major government agency helping the TNCs to send their capital abroad. Sometime in the early 1980s, Commerce invited 120,000 businessmen to an expo in Mexico City to learn how to move their manufacturing plants to Mexico and to ship the almost finished product back to the U.S. to avoid tariff payments. This outraged Joe Kolter, Democratic Congressman from Pennsylvania. He warned that the expo will teach American corporations how to maximize their profits by using low-wage Mexican labor to replace American labor.[42]

The U.S. Agency for International Development (U.S. AID) gave over $102 million dollars to the Salvadorean Foundation for Economic and Social Development (FUSADES). In a 1991 funding agreement, U.S. AID instructed FUSADES to 'pursue a proactive direct and systematic effort, involving direct contact with targeted U.S. firms to convince them to explore opportunities in El Salvador.'

What were those opportunities? Salvadorean women "can be hired for 33 cents an hour and are known for their industriousness, reliability, and quick learning."[43]

The U.S. AID informed the TNCs that "Rumania is a likely place for foreign investment opportunities. Rumania has a dependable low-cost and controlled labor force... with its well-trained workers eager to learn advanced western technology and techniques...Internal, political and economic risks are minimal."[44]

By September 1992, the Reagan and Bush administrations had spent $1.3 billion in taxpayer's money to promote the export of factories to Latin America, where workers are paid as little as 26 cents an hour. That $1.3 billion was used to fund 93 investment promotion groups in Central America and the Caribbean. The groups' instructions were to target U.S. firms and provide them with incentives to relocate their operations from the U.S. to the Caribbean region. U.S. corporations were offered industrial parks built with taxpayers' money, an ample supply of workers desperately in need of jobs, a union-free environment, the lowest wages in the world, one hundred percent tax exemption, duty-free imports to the U.S., cash for corporate chief executive officers to inspect relocation sites and low-interest loans subsidized by U.S. taxes to help with start-up costs.[45]

Consequences of Job Exports for Working People

The worst consequence of job exports for working people in the U.S. is the fact that the overwhelming number of those jobs, both potential and actual, are relatively well-paid manufacturing and unionized jobs. U.S. workers, blue collar as well as white collar, who have been displaced by plant closings have been compelled to take jobs in the service sector where the average wage is 77 percent or less of the average manufacturing wage.[46] This movement of workers from the manufacturing sector to the service sector has increased the supply of workers in the service sector, allowing employers in the service sector to further depress wages for those workers.[47] From 1973 to 1993, writes Edmund Brown, American trade with other nations doubled, but the value of American paychecks fell 18 percent. From 1983 to 1993, the number of young men working full time who earn only a poverty wage has increased 100 percent.[48] Also, because service jobs often do not pay enough to support a family, many service workers are compelled to work overtime or to take a second, or even third job, thus taking time away from parents to create a positive home environment.

Moreover, because the prices of goods imported from sweatshop factories in foreign countries are generally lower than those produced in the U.S., the imported goods have a competitive advantage over domestically produced goods. This puts downward pressure on the wages of production workers and those without college degrees. Such workers account for 72.7 percent of the workforce. But those are not the only burdens borne by working people due to the export of jobs.

By threatening to shift their operations to other countries, corporations pressure their workers to accept lower wages and benefits. Such threats also have a chilling effect on attempts to organize workers in unions. Additionally, when plants are shut down and large numbers of workers lose their jobs, their communities are robbed of income and their local governments are deprived of an adequate tax base to fund community needs. Taxpayers everywhere are left to pay the tax bills. All this time the TNCs use their freedom to go all over the globe to shelter their profits. The final outcome of such developments is that whole communities like South Central Los Angeles; Camden, New Jersey; Flint, Michigan; Toledo, Ohio; to name only a few, have suffered continuing economic and social decline.[49]

"More serious," observes Ronald Kwan, "the export of capital and production limits the ability of all governments to control their economies. The removal of controls over what corporations do with their money limits government's ability to spend on social benefits to families, the unemployed and retirees. During the recession of the early 1990s, for example, U.S. policy makers found themselves boxed in because the Federal government could not lower interest rates too far for it would risk pushing the owners of capital to flee to countries offering higher interest rates. Further, says Kwan, "because now such a high proportion of the profits of the TNCs come from their foreign operations, they have fewer long-term interests with the U.S. communities in which they operate than they once did. The TNCs now have less stake in a community's infrastructure, education, training or health care. And they are less concerned with maintaining good relations with their employees. In fact, if the local community or their employees do not come up with direct or indirect subsidies or contract concessions, the TNCs can and often do threaten to shift production elsewhere."[50]

Chapter Ten

Mergers and Acquisitions as a Cause of Mass Unemployment

There is yet another, mostly hidden, way in which mass unemployment is created. In this chapter, we shall first track the various phases of a process that has been transforming competitive capitalism into an essentially monopolistic capitalism. We shall then tell why businessmen strive to eliminate competition, and then see how monopolies have contributed to mass unemployment for America's workers.

A brief sketch of the successful efforts by business people to eliminate competition

Up to the time of America's Civil War in 1861-1865, the typical economic unit was the small firm such as family farms, artisans and small workshops. Most of the retailers were mom and pop stores. After the Civil War and with the opening up of the West, the markets for goods and services increased enormously and so did prospects for increased profits. The competition for those profits became a driving force for businessmen. Intense competition with rivals, both domestic and foreign, compelled businessmen to lower their prices. Dramatically reduced prices resulted in disastrously reduced profits, which culminated in the first great depression of 1873 to the mid-1890s. Each businessman, facing price competition, tried to undercut his rival's prices, to outsell him and generally, to destroy him economically.[1] So as this process escalated, smaller businesses were swallowed by bigger ones and the bigger ones were swallowed by still bigger ones.

From this profit depression, which ruined numerous businesses, the surviving businessmen learned the obvious lesson. Price competition must be controlled, and if possible, entirely eliminated. For the first time in American history, many business people joined together, creating various forms of organizations to control and eliminate price competition.[2]

Several forms of business organizations were tried, but the one that emerged triumphant was the merger. Mergers occurred in several waves. The first wave occurred shortly after the first Great Depression. By the late 1890s, many firms merged under one ownership and identity. Between 1897 and 1905, in the first spectacular wave to combine ownership, over 5,300 industrial firms came under the control of 318 of the most advanced and powerful corporations.[3]

During the second wave, which occurred in the 1920s and the early 1930s, a total of 11,852 firms were swallowed. In 1929 alone, 2,750 or 43 percent of all public utility firms disappeared into mergers. Also during this wave, there were numerous bank mergers. A total of 1,060 bank mergers occurred between 1919 and 1930. Between 1930 and 1931, a total of 1,567 banks underwent mergers.[4]

The third wave, which began in the 1940s, did not subside until the early 1970s.[5] From 1964 to 1966, there were 293 mergers, and between 1967 and 1970, there were 530 mergers. In 1968 alone, the 200 largest industrial companies acquired 94 large firms with assets worth $8 billion.[6]

By 1972, this process evolved into the creation of giant corporations dominating huge sectors of production and sales. As of that year, the 500 largest industrial corporations controlled 65 percent of the sales of all industrial firms, 75 percent of their total profits and 75 percent of total industrial employment.[7]

Between 1975 and 1981, the number of acquisitions accelerated. In 1975, there were only fourteen mergers involving companies worth $100 million or more and involved a total of $11.8 billion. In 1978, there were eighty mergers involving companies worth $100 million or more and involved a total of $34.2 billion.[8]

The fourth wave of mergers occurred between 1981 and 1989. What distinguished this merger wave was the large size of the companies acquired. In 1981, during the Reagan administration, big business engaged in an orgy of mergers and acquisitions. More than $82 billion were spent on 2,395 mergers, an amount nearly 50 percent greater than the previous yearly high.

What the Wall Street Journal called the biggest monopolization wave ever to sweep across the country occurred in 1984. During the first nine months of that year more than 125 companies each worth more than $100 million were gobbled up by others. Eleven companies worth more than $1 billion were also swallowed. Altogether 1900 companies valued at $103 billion merged or were acquired. The previous high mark was $83 billion for all of 1981.[9]

By the 1990s, with the emergence of transnational mergers, all previous records were broken. Between 1990 and 1997, mergers and acquisitions gobbled up $2,908,000,000 of the nation's wealth. During 1997, a new yearly high was reached when $698 billion was spent on acquisitions and mergers.[10] Well-known economist Robert Samuelson called the mergers between 1994 and 2000 a "mysterious merger frenzy." He wrote that "Despite the uncertainties, something momentous is clearly happening. The numbers suggest no other conclusion. In 1999, U.S. corporate mergers and acquisitions approached $1.5 trillion. Since 1994 the cumulative mergers and acquisitions exceed $5 trillion. These figures cover only mergers involving U.S. firms as buyer or seller. Once cross-border mergers were rare. No more. In 1999, they totaled $720 billion."[11]

Why Do Firms Acquire or Merge With Other Firms?

Before we explore the motives that propel corporations to acquire and merge with other corporations, it may be rewarding to trace the historical background of the idea of capitalism as a competitive system. As the narrative progresses, we will see how a system, which was originally competitive, has over time evolved into an essentially non-competitive one even though the spokespeople of capitalism still incessantly sing the praises of competition and its uses to trumpet the glories of capitalism. First, we should be aware that capitalism as a system of production and distribution has not always existed. Capitalism evolved about five hundred years ago from feudalism and has been going through many different stages ever since.

The first stage of what became a very long journey was marked, among other things, by the conquest and pillage of the Americas in the 16th century. This was accompanied by the decimation of many of the indigenous peoples of the American continents. This pillage gave birth to capitalism's second stage, that of merchant and manufacturing capitalism. For example, foreign trade conducted by merchants increased tenfold between 1610 and 1640. In the area of manufacturing, by 1640, some coalfields in England were producing 10,000-25,000 tons of coal per year. Just one century ago no more than a few hundred tons were produced.[12]

Merchant and manufacturing capitalism soon developed into a robust industrial capitalism. By the 18th century, due to an explosion in industrial technology, England became the world's leading industrial nation.

"During the second half of the 18th century," writes historian Michel Beaud, "interest in technical innovations became unusually intensive. For a hundred years prior to 1760, the number of patents issued during each decade reached 102 only once. During the following thirty-year period, 1760-1789, the average number of patents issued increased from 205 in the 1760s to 294 in the 1770s, and to 447 in the 1780s.[13]

By the mid-1700s, many of England's cities were humming with industrial activity taking place in hundreds of 'manufactories.' Manufactories were centers of production in which a businessman owned the building, the production equipment and the raw materials, and hired wage laborers to do the work. Workers toiled mainly at handicraft production prior to the mechanized assembly line technology.[14]

It was against this background of enormous industrial advances that Adam Smith wrote The Wealth of Nations, a book regarded by many of the ideologues of the business class as its Bible. Adam Smith saw that the manufactories were in competition with one another. Such competition, he concluded, was beneficial for society because it would compel the owners of the manufactories to lower prices. But he also observed that, "People of the same trade seldom meet together, even for merriment and diversion, but the conversation ends in a conspiracy against the public or in some contrivance to raise prices." Smith further observed that, "The interest of the dealers, however, in any particular branch of trade or manufacture, is always in some respects different from and even opposite to that of the public...To narrow the competition is always the interest of dealers...But to narrow the competition must always be against...[the interests of the public] and can serve only to enable the dealers, by raising their profits above what they naturally would be, to levy, for their own benefit, an absurd tax upon the rest of their fellow citizens."[15] What Smith meant by 'to narrow the competition' was the compelling need of businessmen to combine in order to increase prices. By "an absurd tax," Smith meant an intolerable burden on consumers in the form of increased prices.

Smith also referred to businessmen as, "an order of men whose interest is never exactly the same with that of the public, [and] who have generally an interest to deceive and even to oppress the public, and who accordingly have, upon many occasions, both deceived and oppressed it."[16]

This tendency to raise prices was noted by Gardiner Means, President Roosevelt's Secretary of Agriculture in 1934. Means noticed that despite the tremendous decline in the sale of goods and services brought about by the Great Depression of the 1930s, many prices did not fall. He therefore distinguished between "market" prices and "administered" prices. Market prices are determined by competition, and when demand for goods and services falls, prices also fall. On the other hand, administered prices are determined by the administrative action of the monopolies and oligopolies. Economists other than Means have called attention to the practice by General Motors, Dupont and other firms of "target return pricing." This practice allows a company first to set a profit target of, say, 20 percent of its investment and then to set its prices at whatever level is required to reap the 20 percent profit target.[17]

What are the motives that drive corporations to merge and acquire other firms?

The most powerful motive that drives businessman, regardless of the size of their businesses, is the anticipation of increased profits. How do mergers increase profits? By acquiring or merging, corporations can reduce all kinds of operating costs. A large firm that expands its size by mergers or acquisitions can demand paying lower prices when buying raw materials in volume. It can also usually obtain credit more cheaply. When a corporation acquires or merges with its suppliers of essential raw materials, or when it gains control of the distribution and retailing network, it is better able to reduce costs of production and also to sell its products cheaper than the competition. In so doing the higher priced producers are eventually driven out of the market.

Whether through mergers with, or acquisitions of, other firms, the growth of some companies comes at the expense of others. This process tends to create the conditions for increasingly greater concentration of companies into monopolistic forms.

So whereas previously, there had been numerous small businesses competing with one another that resulted in driving prices and profits down, now large conglomerates maintain and even raise prices and profits.[18]

An example of how mergers and acquisition result in greatly increased prices and profits is the oil industry. In 1979, Mobil Oil spent $800 million or 37 percents of its global capital budget to swallow a competitor, General Crude. A few years ago Mobil bought out Montgomery Ward and The Container Corporation of America for $1.8 billion. Gulf Oil took over the model city of Reston, Virginia. About a decade ago, some "major oil companies took over or bought into the largest coal companies. Others moved into copper mining and chemicals. These corporations have long since acquired fleets of tankers, many registered in Liberia or Panama, to escape union contracts and U.S. taxes.[19]

The mergers and acquisitions of the oil companies produced a profits bonanza. During the third quarter of 1979, the 18 largest oil companies reported $6 billion in profits, an increase of 103% over the same period a year earlier. These oil giants made $15 billion in the first nine months of 1979, an increase of 71% over a year earlier. By comparison, the profits of 833 non-energy corporations rose less than 9% for the third quarter and only 17% for the first nine months."[20]

The Consequences of Mergers and Acquisitions for America's Working People

Mergers and acquisitions have many adverse consequences for America's working people. Those consequences include mass layoffs; increase in the prices working people have to pay for life's necessities; growing inflation which reduces the value of worker's wages and salaries, and less obviously but no less insidiously, the rapid erosion of democracy.

Here we will limit the discussion of the consequences to mass layoffs. Pro-establishment politicians and economists proclaim a new era of rising productivity and more jobs whenever they publicize imminent mass layoffs as a result of new mergers. Those who justify new mergers claim that they will bring forth greater efficiency, increased ability to meet foreign competition and that in the long run, all will benefit.[21] The fact is that no agency, government or otherwise, is assigned the job of tracking the number of workers laid off as a consequence of mergers and acquisitions. Any data that exists comes from sources that mention layoffs only as part of their other concerns. So we learn that the AOL-Time Warner merger has resulted in the dismissal of 12,000 workers.[22] More than 100,000 jobs were lost in the banking industry alone in the rash of mergers that accelerated in 1989.[23]

When Exxon Corporation acquired Mobil Corporation, 9,000 jobs were lost. When British Petroleum merged with Amoco, they planned to shed 6,000 jobs.[24]

Family farms are fast disappearing, due partly to the merger movement. Since 1982, the U.S. has lost 85 farmers a day in a rural economy that is already so precarious that family farmers now derive over 88% of their household income from off-farm activities. "Mergers, acquisitions and alliances are squelching competition in the market place," said Leland Swenson, President of the National Farmers Union. "It is an epidemic sweeping the entire industry, including the seed, chemical, transportation, livestock and grain sectors. The mother of all mergers – Cargill's purchase of Continental Grain – has far-reaching implications for the future direction of crop production and independent family farming."[25]

Cargill's purchase of Continental's Grain operations is expected to result in the closing and merging of many local grain elevators that served as a vital part of rural economies. Grain elevators provided badly needed jobs, wages and revenues, and their demise was expected to seriously erode, if not irreparably damage, the health of many of our nation's rural communities.

In an article entitled, *Concern about Mergers in Health Plans*, Milt Freudenheim wrote that, "Doctors and hospitals are increasingly concerned...that the health insurance industry is rapidly whittling itself down to a few giant companies that dominate the health care system of some of the country's biggest cities." In only five years, six health insurers have scooped up a dozen companies. Only Aetna, Cigna, United Health Care, Foundation Health Systems, Pacificare and Wellpoint Health Networks have survived. "This merger trend," writes Freudenheim, "is also raising questions about the cost and availability of care to millions of patients and their employers."[26]

Aetna made two billion dollar deals to swallow Prudential Health Care, the fifth largest for profit health insurer, while it was still digesting its July purchase of NYL-Care, the eleventh largest insurer. Freudenheim has said little about the layoffs that such mergers have left in their wake. But to catch a glimpse of how mergers and acquisition in the health care field affect working people, *Labor Notes* reported that in the [merger] process, registered nurses' jobs are being cut dramatically. According to the

American Nurses Association, a 1994 survey of 1800 hospitals showed that more than two-thirds of the hospitals had reduced registered nurse (RN) positions in the previous year. A survey by the Boston College School of Nursing in the same year found that one tragic consequence of this elimination of RN jobs was that 15 cases of patient deaths were attributed to inadequate nurse staffing. No such cases were reported when the same survey was conducted in 1989.[27]

A classic case of what happened to working people when a giant corporation was merely threatened with an acquisition occurred in 1986 with Safeway Stores Inc. Safeway laid off 63,000 managers and workers. The majority of those who were laid off were re-employed, but usually at lower wages. Many thousands wound up either unemployed or in part-time jobs. A survey of former Safeway employees in Dallas found that nearly 60% still had not found full-time employment more than a year after the layoffs. One Dallas worker, a Mr. White, had been a Safeway trucker for nearly 30 years. In 1988, one year after he had been laid off, he told his wife he loved her, he then locked himself in the bathroom, loaded his 22 caliber hunting rifle and blew his brains out. Patricia Vasquez, a 14 year systems analyst and famous for her refusal to take off for lunch break, packed her service citations in a cardboard box and left looking pale and drawn. The next morning her two young children found their single mother on the bathroom floor, dead of a heart attack. Another employee, Mr. Quigley, came home and told his wife that he was going to be fired. His wife, a diabetic who had been in good health for years, was hospitalized and died just months after her husband's dismissal.

In addition to Mr. White's suicide, at least 20 others tried to kill themselves. One was Bill Mayfield Jr., a Safeway mechanic. He slashed his wrist, then shot himself in the stomach, but survived because the bullet just missed his vital organs. No matter where the laid off workers landed, many saw their wages drop from $12.09 to $6.50 an hour. Kay Seabolt, a human resources supervisor, had one incident seared into her memory. A tattered middle-aged man, who served for many years in the Safeway bread plant, made his way to Seabolt's desk with a slow, wincing limp. Apologizing for his appearance, he explained that he had just walked six miles, his car had been repossessed and he was living in a homeless shelter. Shortly after this incident Kay Seabolt, her elevated status notwithstanding , she, her husband Ron and their daughter were all given pink slips on the same day.[27a]

Similar devastation occurred in the lives of working people when, in 1986, Sir James Goldsmith, a European corporate raider, attempted an unsuccessful acquisition of Goodyear Tire Corporation. To buy back the Goldsmith shares in the company, Goodyear sank into a $2.6 billion debt for which it had to pay $200 million a year in interest. To pay off the debt, Goodyear was compelled to fire 680 employees in Akron, Ohio and to close three of its other tire plants. Goodyear closed its Kelly-Springfield plant in Cumberland and laid off 1,675 employees. In Toronto, Ontario, Goodyear, gave pink slips to 1,400 unionized tire workers and roughly 200 white collar workers. In Goodyear's Windsor, Vermont, tire plant, 300 unionized workers and an unknown number of white collar workers lost their jobs.[28]

In the summer of 1986, the Wickes Corporation attempted to acquire the Owens-Corning Fiberglass Corporation (OCF). To beat back the Wickes takeover, OCF incurred an incredible $2.6 billion debt. To pay off this huge debt, OCF closed its plant in Barrington, New Jersey, laying off 800 unionized workers and 200 management employees. OCF reduced its range and scope of operations and within months, its work force dropped from 28,000 to 13,000. Significant too is the 50% funding cut in its Granville, Ohio, research center.[29]

A still sharper comment on the effects of the takeover frenzy of the late 1970s and the 1980s was made by Walter B Kissinger, himself a prominent businessman. "It is of no interest or concern to these [takeover] individuals that they touch the lives of tens of thousands of workers who may become unemployed; that they destroy the careers of dedicated individuals who have devoted their lives to building a company, that they frequently destroy communities, that they undermine the vitality and creativeness of a company, and that they hoodwink the small shareholder who has little say in the matter and little knowledge of what is going on."[30]

Chapter Eleven

Imported Labor as a Cause of Mass Unemployment

It has been estimated that by 2004, 9.1 million illegal immigrants are in the U.S., as well as between 1 and 2 million persons on long-term temporary visas, mainly students and guest workers (not included are aliens in prisons and nursing homes). To understand why many immigrants are imported into the U.S., it is necessary to see the issue from the standpoint of the employer class.

In 1998, the American Meat Institute and a group of corporate trade associations in industries employing large numbers of immigrant workers created the Essential Worker Immigrant Coalition (EWIC). In a very short time, the EWIC grew to include 36 of the most powerful employer associations led by the U.S. Chamber of Commerce. The EWIC included the National Association of Chain Drug Stores which counted Wal-Mart among its members, the American Healthcare Association, the American Hotel and Lodging Association, the National Council of Chain Restaurants, the National Restaurant Association, and the National Retail Federation. Also among the members is the violently anti-union Associated General Builders and Contractors All of the members of those groups depend on a workforce almost entirely without benefits and working at close to minimum wage.[1]

Many of the illegal immigrants come to the U.S. through orders placed by corporate managers with smugglers for a specific number of able bodies to be delivered.

"For corporate America employing illegal aliens at wages so low few citizens could afford to take the jobs, is great for profits and stockholders. That is why the payrolls of so many businesses – meat packers, poultry processors, landscape firms, construction companies, office cleaning firms, and corner convenience stores, among others – are jammed with illegal immigrants. And companies are rarely, if ever, punished for it."[2]

Truley Ponder, one of Tyson's managers who pleaded guilty to hiring illegal aliens, describes why corporations prefer to use illegal aliens. Tyson Foods, Inc. is one of the world's largest processors and marketers of chicken, beef, and pork.[3] According to documents filed as part of the Ponder's guilty plea, the U.S. Attorney's office noted that "Ponder would have preferred ...to hire 'local people' [read native-born workers] but this was not feasible in light of the low wages that Tyson paid...Ponder made numerous requests for pay increases...above and beyond what the company routinely allowed. But Tyson's corporate management...rejected his requests for pay increases for production workers. Needless to say," writes the Time reporter, "hiring had benefits for Tyson...A government consultant estimated that the company saved millions of dollars in wages, benefits, and other costs."[4]

The massive flow of illegal immigrants from Mexico and other Latin American countries is a relatively recent phenomenon. That flow has been caused by the so-called free trade policies pushed by U.S. corporations and supported by both Republican and Democratic administrations. Those policies allow U.S. corporations unfettered freedom to export their agricultural

products and other goods and services to Latin American countries where they are sold at prices with which Latino farmers
and many businesses cannot compete. Consequently, many of
them lose their source of living. In desperation and in order to
survive, many of them, their adult children and sometimes entire families trek North in a dangerous and desperate attempt
to find work.

The very same causes and consequences suffered by Latin
Americans have been experienced by many of America's family
farms and small businesses. They too have been unable to compete with the cheaper prices charged for the goods and services of the large corporations, thus compelling many of their sons
and daughters to leave the farms for the urban centers where
much better prospects exists for earning a living.

Similar processes, though perhaps on a smaller scale have
been occurring in many countries of the third world – processes
that have stolen the livelihood of numerous small business and
working people, and thus driving them in desperation towards
America's shores for the chance of gainful employment.

The Impact of Immigration on Native-born Workers

A study published in October 2004 found the following:

- Between March of 2000 and 2004, the number of unemployed adult natives increased by 2.3 million while the number of employed adult immigrants increased by 2.3 million.
- Half of the 2.3 million increase in immigrant employment
  since 2000 is estimated to be from illegal immigration.

- In addition to a growth in unemployment, the number of working-age (18-64) natives who left the labor-force entirely increased by four million since 2000.
- Even over the last year the same general pattern holds. Of the 900,000 net increase in jobs between March 2003 and 2004, two-thirds went to immigrant workers, even though they account for only 15% of all adult workers.
- In just the last year, 1.2 million working-age natives left the labor force, and say that they are not even trying to find a job.
- Immigrant job gains have occurred throughout the labor market, with more than two-thirds of their employment gains among workers who have at least a high school degree.
- There is little evidence that immigrants take only jobs Americans don't want. Even those occupations with the highest concentrations of new immigrants still employ millions of native-born workers.[5]

An earlier study came up with the following findings:

- By increasing the supply of labor between 1980 and 2000, immigration reduced the average annual earnings of native-born workers by an estimated $1,700 or roughly 4%.
- Among natives without a high school education, who roughly correspond to the poorest tenth of the workforce, the estimated impact was even larger, reducing their wages by 7.4%.
- The 10 million native-born workers without a high school degree face the most competition from immigrants, as do the eight million younger natives with only a high school education and 12 million younger college graduates.

- The negative effect on native-born Black and Hispanic workers is significantly larger than on Whites because a much larger share of minorities are in direct competition with immigrants.[6]

How Many High Tech Workers Are Legally Imported

As of 2001, there were a total of 713,000 foreign high tech workers employed by U.S. companies in this country. There are two categories of high tech workers imported from overseas. One category, the H-1B visas accounted for 384,000 high tech foreign workers in the U.S. The other category, the L-1 visas, had 329,000 workers. Most of these foreign workers come from India, Philippines, China, and Taiwan.[7] India, in particular, has had a huge investment in educational infrastructure. It has increased its number of active scientific and technical personnel 200 times from 188,000 in 1950 to 3.8 Million in 1990. They were brought into the U.S. thanks to two laws enacted by Congress. Under the first law, H-1B visa scheme, companies are not permitted to use it to displace American workers and must pay H-1B workers the prevailing U.S. wage. Employers must also file detailed documents with the Labor Department which closely monitors H-1B visa holders. The L-1 visa scheme, is only slightly supervised by the State Department. No provisions exist against displacing American workers, or requirements to pay prevailing wages. The L-1 scheme also allows foreign information technology (IT) firms to file blanket petitions for ongoing approval to bring multiple aliens into the U.S.[8]

Why are they brought in, and under what pretext

Many companies wishing to reduce labor costs use the L-1 visa scheme "to dump high-paid workers in favor of cheaper workers from abroad. As a result, many companies are subcontracting thousands of jobs to outsourcing companies, such as Tata, Inforsys Technologies, and Wipro Technologies – the three largest Indian software servicing companies, and all of which are using more L-1s. Among those using such IT contractors are Bank of America, Dell Computer, General Electric, Merrill Lynch, and Siemens."[9] These companies have lobbied Congress for those laws that allow the import foreign labor saying that they cannot find Americans to fill those jobs. But "recent layoffs at companies, such as Hewlett-Packard, Intel, Motorola, and Lucent Technologies, have cast doubt on industry claims of a labor shortage. Last year [1998], a study by the employment firm Challenger, Grey, and Christmas calculated that 21 major high tech companies had laid off more than a 120,000 workers over a period of six months."[10]

One of the visa programs, the H-1B, "has become a major means of circumventing the costs of paying skilled American workers, or the costs of training them" testified then-Secretary of Labor, Robert Reich, in 1995.[11] Patricia Fluno, one of the many displaced high tech workers, was shocked when she found out that she and 11 colleagues in the Lake Mary (Fla.), officers of Siemens were being replaced by techies brought in by Tata. Fluno said that her Siemens supervisors told her "the Indian employee who replaced her earns just one-third of her $98,000 a year."[12] Businesses will inevitably exploit loopholes in our immigration policy to seek cheaper labor.

Chapter Twelve

The Federal Reserve Bank as a Creator of Mass Unemployment

The law that established the Federal Reserve Bank in 1913 was written largely by the nation's bankers themselves. However, the present almost unrestrained power of the Federal Reserve Bank did not develop without a struggle.

During the last two decades of the 19th century, a number of organizations, including the Populist movement, the Farmers' Alliance, the People's Party, the Farmer's Union and organized labor, called for some degree of democratic control over monetary policy which was controlled exclusively by bankers. Farmers were most hurt by the high cost of operating their farms, and they were at the forefront of the movement for lower interest rates. Interest rates in the South and the Midwest at that time ranged from fifteen to thirty percent, and credit was difficult to get. The demands for reform posed a serious threat to the banks. Faced with this threat, bankers closed ranks and through their influence in Congress succeeded in setting up a system that benefited their interests. The 1913 Federal Reserve Act passed by Congress created a banking system, which over time became totally isolated from any pressure from working people and their needs.[1]

We generally think of money as a device with which we are paid for our work and which we spend or save for future needs. But not many of us are aware that money is much more than that. It has become a product and like any other product it is bought and sold, lent and borrowed. In fact it has become a product that now dominates every other. Those individuals, businesses and institutions which possess huge amounts of money now have almost total control over our economy and thus over important aspects of our lives. Large banks, which control most of our nation's money, make huge profits by borrowing our money at low interest rates in savings and other accounts, and lending it at much higher interest rates to individual borrowers or businesses. When banks and other lending institutions lend money, they expect that the money plus interest paid back to them to be worth the same or more than the money they originally lent. Therefore, banks and other lenders fear money inflation more than anything else because it reduces the worth of money over time.

So what do the banks and other lenders do to maintain or increase the value of the money they lend out? That task is taken care of by the Federal Reserve Bank. The Fed, as it has been nicknamed, serves the interests of all the nation's moneylenders. When the Fed raises interest rates, the borrowing of money becomes more expensive. When interest rates rise, borrowers tend to wait for interest rates to drop before borrowing to finance a business, a home, a car or any other item. Also, people who wish to borrow to maintain or expand their businesses would tend to hold off for the same reason. Thus when businesses are unable to sell enough autos, houses and other high-priced goods, or when they hold off borrowing to maintain or expand their businesses, many of them go bankrupt or retrench. In both instances, they lay off all or some of their workers. Millions of workers suddenly find themselves without a job. The layoff epidemic triggers pervasive fear and anxiety among the many workers whose jobs may be the next to be cut. Those who are still employed fear negotiating for better pay and working conditions and many may also agree to reduced wages or benefits or both in exchange for job security. The net result of lower labor costs is an increase in profits without an increase in the price of the manufactured goods. Because many businesses borrow heavily from lenders, their increased profits allow them to pay back their loans to the banks at dollars that have retained or increased their value.

How Do Banks and Other Lenders Fare When the Fed Raises Interest Rates?

High interest rates remove wealth from the pockets of working people into the coffers of the wealthy. This was never more so than during the Carter and Reagan administrations. During those years, the high interest rates introduced by Paul Volker, Chairman of the Federal Reserve Bank, shifted wealth dramatically from working people to the owners of large amounts of capital.

From the 1930s to the 1960s, wages and salaries accounted for about 66 percent of all personal income. By 1983, wages and salaries dropped to 60.7 percent of total personal income, and fell to 59.5 percent the following year. From 1979 to 1983, personal income derived solely from interest grew by more than 70 percent, an increase of $158 billion. When dividends from stocks are added, the share of lenders virtually doubled: from 11 percent in 1979 to 20 percent in 1984 and this was due primarily to government actions.[2]

According to the U.S. Census, from 1980 to 1983, families in the top 20 percent of the economic ladder enjoyed real increases in their after tax household incomes, while the bottom 80 percent actually lost income. The high interest rates were especially profitable for the holders of large number of bonds. From 1981 to 1985 returns from their loans averaged 18.5 percent a year. For bondholders, that rate of return was the most lucrative in the 20th century.[3]

To justify the raising of interest rates, the Fed almost always conjures up the dragon of inflation. In one of his public announcements, Volker warned that, "The standard of living of the average American has to decline. I don't think you can escape that."[4] But as every statistician knows, averages always conceal gross inequalities.

As noted earlier, fighting inflation by raising interest rates has the effect of enriching money lenders on the one hand, and of unleashing mass layoffs of working people on the other. But as noted earlier, mass layoffs also intimidate workers whose jobs were not cut. And as mentioned earlier, much to the delight of lenders, the fear of being the next to be laid off induces workers to work harder and longer, thus increasing production at lower labor costs. Thus the value of the dollar is maintained or increased. But Federal Reserve chairmen, whether Paul Volker or Allan Greenspan, never as much as hint at the real and root causes of inflation.

A Closer Look at the Fate of Workers When Interest Rates Are Raised

To get a picture of what happens to working people when the Federal Reserve Bank raises interest rates, let us have a look at those consequences during the years 1981-1986 when Ronald Reagan presided over one of the worst periods of mass unemployment in modern American history. In his superb book, *Secrets of the Temple*, William Greider gives us a glimpse of the experiences of workers who lost their jobs during the Reagan recession.[5]

The vast steel mills along the Monongahela River outside Pittsburgh had once employed 28,000 basic steelworkers at premium industrial wages – what Robert Craven, another laid-off steel worker, described as "Big Bucks." After the spate of steep interest rate increases by the Fed, only 6,000 jobs were left. Grieder tells of Carl Redwood Jr., a young steel worker who, after being laid off from his steel mill, went from one disappointing job to another, first as security guard, then as a meter maid issuing parking tickets, and then as counselor at a day camp.

Another laid off worker, Arnie Leibowitz, said he tried to commit suicide by jumping into a river and ended up in a state mental hospital for treatment. Greider writes that everyone seemed to know someone who had attempted suicide or had succeeded, and that the county coroner reported that suicides were up 11 percent.

In union-dominated heavy industry, between 1979 and 1984 an estimated 5.1 million workers were permanently displaced by plant closings. About half that number were cut from the manufacturing sector, and the Bureau of Labor Statistics estimated that only about 60 percent of those workers found new jobs. Even when the unemployment rate was reduced from 9.6 percent to just above 7 percent, 8.4 million were officially unemployed and another 1.3 million were described as "discouraged" workers who had stopped registering at the unemployment office. Another 5.7 million workers like Carl Redwood and Robert Craven were forced to work part time at temporary jobs with wages far below their normal incomes. "In all," comments Greider, "the voiceless minority – those who had nobody to represent them – totaled more than 15 million citizens."[6]

The unemployed were lucky if all they lost were their jobs. Many of them also lost their homes because they could not keep up with their mortgage rates. When one such family, Elizabeth Laird and her husband, were four months behind in their payments, they filed for bankruptcy and became renters. In despair, Mrs. Laird said, "I want to say, 'God, I know you are building character in me but sometimes I want to ask, how much character do I need?'"[7]

By 1984, the Veterans Administration held 29,000 foreclosed homes. In 1985, the mortgage insurance industry paid out $425 million on foreclosures, three times the number of homes lost in 1983. By 1985, mortgage delinquencies had reached the highest level in 22 years, the Mortgage Bankers Association announced.[8]

By 1983, workers in most sectors of the heavy industries who had not lost their jobs saw their wages pushed downwards. Steelworkers were compelled to accept wage cuts and wage freezes. Autoworkers gave up substantial wage and benefit improvements in new contracts at Ford and General Motors. Coal miners settled for a $1.40 per hour raise, compared to the $3.60 raise in their previous contract. Airline machinists and other airline unions accepted wage freezes and a two-tier pay scale which meant that younger newer members would be paid less than older members for the same work. Oil workers, facing the closing of 83 refineries, settled for a 20 cent hourly pay increase at Gulf Oil.[9] In 1983, altogether about 1.1 million union workers were compelled to accept pay cuts or freezes. That trend continued at almost the same pace in subsequent years, and strikes and work stoppages subsided to the lowest level since World War II.[10]

What Are the Real and Root Causes of Inflation?

The spokespersons of the corporate-investor class never tire of accusing working people, especially unionized workers, of wanting better wages and benefits, which, they say, is the prime cause of the money inflation that plagues our society. On the other hand, a deafening silence reigns about inflation's deepest causes.

Nothing is ever said about the inflationary impact of the bloated military budget, nor about the inflated prices that cor-

porate monopolies and oligopolies charge for their products
and services. The huge tax cuts and other tax privileges to the
corporations and the wealthy are not mentioned either, and
they, like the military budget, deplete the federal treasury and
thus cause horrendous inflationary deficits which in turn compels the federal government to print bails of money.

Nothing is more insidious than military spending and wars
in the creation of inflation. Inflation results from pumping too
much money into the economy relative to the supply of available goods. Wars and other military expenditures are generally
financed by money borrowed from financiers and financial institutions. Before the Vietnam War, inflation was low, but afterwards, inflation increased substantially. That war, like the others
before it, required increased arms production. Arms manufacturers compete with manufacturers producing civilian goods for
raw materials and other resources. As raw materials become
scarcer, their prices increase. The increase in production costs
due to the increase in the cost of raw materials allows manufacturers as well as providers of raw materials to raise their prices.

The cost of arms spending results in an increase of the federal budget deficit. Whereas from 1960 to 1964 the average
yearly deficit was $4 billion, by 1968, it had reached $25 billion.
The government borrowed heavily to pay for the war. This was
just one more factor in pushing up the rate of inflation.

Whereas wars have proven to be a bonanza for arms manufacturers, the steep price increases and consequent inflation
triggered by war has also helped to erode the standard of living for most working people. The following chart shows the
connection between wars and inflation.

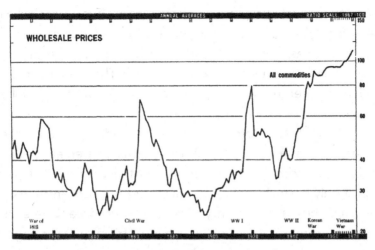

WHOLESALE PRICES

Source: *Historical Chart Book*, 1971, Board of Governors, Federal Reserve System, p. 101. War captions added.

As the chart shows, the major inflationary periods in the U.S. occurred during America's wars and their aftermath – from the war of 1812, to the Civil War, to the First and Second World Wars and on to the Vietnam War.

Another major cause of inflation is the bloated prices monopolistic and oligopolistic corporations charge for their goods and services. The spokespersons of corporate America never stop telling us that our economic system is a free market system. They claim that it is the consumer that determines the prices of goods and services. Their theory says that if too many consumers wish to purchase a certain product that is in short supply, the price of that product will inevitably go up. But if there is an oversupply of that product, its price will inevitably go down. Economists have called this theory the law of supply and demand.

That law was true in the past, and is still true where there are numerous small businesses producing the same product or services. But in order to sell enough goods or services to make a profit or just to avoid a loss, small businesses must reduce their prices to attract customers away from other businesses selling the same product. The competition between numerous sellers force prices downwards and that was the typical economic reality for all of America's earlier history.[11] That all changed in the late 19th century when the first monopolies and oligopolies emerged.

By 1972, the 500 largest corporations had gained control of 65 percent of the sales of all industrial firms, 75 percent of their total profits and 75 percent of total industrial employment. And this list only partially reveals the extent of the concentration of the ownership of this country's manufacturing base. One economist wrote that in their respective industries, the four largest corporations had, by 1975, controlled 99 percent of the automobiles, 96 percent of the aluminum, 80 percent of the cigarettes and 72 percent of the soaps and detergents produced nationally.[12]

What happens to prices when ownership of production is so highly concentrated? And how do those prices affect inflation? Consider the following facts. In 1934, Gardiner Means, the Secretary of Agriculture, noticed that despite the steep decline in demand [purchases] brought about by the Depression of 1929-1933, many prices did not fall. He therefore drew a distinction between "market prices" and "administered prices." Market prices are determined by competition, so when demand falls, prices also fall.

Administered prices are determined, not by competition in the market place, but by the actions of monopolies. Other economists have called attention to the practice of General Motors, DuPont and other firms to what is known as "target return pricing." Under this method, a company first sets a profit target, say 20 percent of its investment. It then fixes its prices at whatever level is required to reap the 20 percent profit target. A Congressional Committee study found that if, during a recession, a monopolistic company loses revenue because of a reduction in sales, it will try to recoup the lost revenue by increasing the prices of its remaining sales so that it can get closer to its target profit rate.[13] When monopolies and oligopolies raise prices to ensure a high profit, both during economic upswings and downturns, consumers and other businesses are compelled to borrow from lenders to pay for higher prices for the goods and services of these giant firms. This has the effect of increasing the supply of money. Excessive increases in the money supply relative to the available goods and services means that more money is needed to purchase an insufficient supply of goods, thus cheapening and therefore inflating the value of money.

A Solution to Inflation Without Creating Unemployment

Economists repeatedly remind us that two-thirds of the economy is driven by consumer spending. It makes sense therefore to increase the income of working people because most of their income is spent rather than saved. In that spirit therefore the following five proposals to solve the problem of inflation without creating mass unemployment were put forward by a distinguished economist.[14]

1. An unqualified guarantee by the Federal government to provide jobs in the public sector as a reliable alternative to the inadequate number of jobs in the private sector. 2. Income maintenance by the federal government at decent levels as a matter of right. 3. A Federal income policy focused on and designed to check the incomes of large corporations and professional societies. 4. Serious federal attention to a tax policy based on a redistribution of wealth so as to create greater financial equality and price stability.

5. In the predictable future, a gradually increasing public and diminishing private sphere of activity which would be a realization of Keynes' vision of a "somewhat comprehensive socialization of investment."

Chapter Thirteen

Recessions as a Cause for Mass Unemployment

One of the major causes of mass unemployment and its attendant misery for many working people is the periodic recessions that afflict all capitalist economies including that of the United States.

The most important and perhaps the key cause of both recessions and depressions in the U.S. has been the great inequality in income and wealth that has almost always existed in the past and that has more recently become outrageously great. That great inequality is between the major owners of all the means of production and distribution that produce and distribute the goods and services and the overwhelming majority of America's working people.[1]

Almost as important as a contributing cause of recessions is the never-ending introduction of advanced technology into both the production and the service industries to replace human labor. Whether a business is owned by a family or by people who own shares in a corporation, all owners are motivated chiefly by a desire for profits. Because the wages and salaries paid to the employees of any business cut into the profits of business owners, few businesses can avoid the temptation to replace their employees with technology that can do the work of many workers far more cheaply. Thus when hundreds of thousands, if not millions, of workers find themselves without jobs, more of the country's total income goes to the owner-investor class and less to the millions of working people. What then happens is that workers are unable to buy all the goods and services they need and which new technology is able to produce in ever greater quantities. It is no wonder, therefore, that to meet their needs, millions of workers feel compelled to resort to the use of the credit card and thus often sink into ever deeper debt. Another consequence of income inequality is the vast expansion of the frenzied efforts by businesses to sell their goods and services. That is why we are exposed to an unending barrage of advertisements and more and more people are sucked into the armies of salespersons and telemarketers.[2]

Another contributory cause of recessions is the export of jobs. It is now the routine practice of hundreds of corporations to send hundreds of thousands of what should have been jobs for American workers to countries where wages are a fraction of what would have been paid here.[3] Thus when fewer workers have the money to buy the available goods and services, many businesses are compelled to cut back on hiring, or worse, are compelled to lay off some or all their workers.

Still another factor that contributes to the creation of recessions is the unending mergers and acquisitions and the numerous layoffs they cause. For whenever such layoffs occur, the working people who end up without jobs or with lower paid jobs have less money to buy the goods and services they need. And therefore, like the other sources of recessions, when working people cannot buy enough of the goods and services they need, many businesses lay off some of their employees or go bankrupt and are then compelled to lay off all their employees.[4]

Most cruel of all the previous causes of recessions is the role of the Federal Reserve Bank. When rising levels of employment increases the bargaining power of working people and thus their wages and benefits, it arouses the fear of inflation among bankers and other lenders. To avoid that inflation, the Federal Reserve Bank deliberately raises interest rates much to the relief of the lenders. But when interest rates are raised high enough, workers and others are discouraged from buying high-ticket items, such as cars and homes. This causes many businesses to go bankrupt or to retrench, resulting in the layoffs of many of their employees.[5]

Periods of Economic Instability

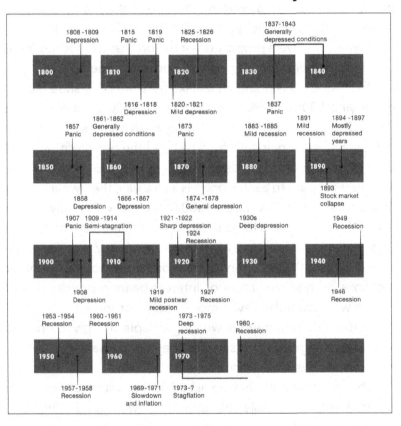

Source: Douglas F. Dowd, Modern Economic Problems in Historical Perspective. 1965, p.143

Recessions have been a recurrent affliction of the U.S. economy. As can be seen from the following chart, since 1808 there have been more than a dozen periods of depressions or recessions.

There were also recessions from 1980 to 1982, from 1990 to 1993, and again from 2001 to 2003.

To repeat: Corporations are not able to sell all the goods and services they produce because workers get too small a proportion of the profits as wages. This does not allow them to buy enough of the available goods and services. On the other hand, the owners receive a proportion of the profits which is too large for them to spend for their normal consumer needs.

To illustrate this point, let us take for example a shoe factory employing 500 workers that produce 100,000 pairs of shoes a week. This is not unlikely given today's advanced state of technology. Say each pair sells for $100 and the net profit, after all operating expenses are deducted, is $30 a pair. If the wages and benefits paid to each worker is $25 a pair, the owner's share of the total net profits will be $500,000 a week. Can any owner, even if he or she has a large family, spend that much money in a week? He or she will more likely invest what they don't need on a daily basis either in opening up more shoe factories in other locations or in some stocks or interest-bearing bonds. This of course will accumulate even more wealth for them.

Not only are numerous working people not given enough to buy all the goods and services they need, many are laid off when recessions hit the economy.

The question then may be asked: Is the system under which we are living compatible with jobs for all who need them? The answer is indicated in some very interesting reports and commentaries that appeared in a couple of publications during the recession of April-May 2001. During the first five months of 2001, the number of workers who lost their jobs totaled 652, 510. These job cuts outstripped the 613, 960 cuts recorded for all of the year 2000.[6] Time Magazine reported that the economy had been shedding 100,000 workers a month since the beginning of the year. However, the New York Times reported that "the stock market treated the bad news as pointing to better times ahead. Prices [of stocks] rose on the major exchanges as investors seemed to conclude that corporate America, in cutting labor costs, was acting to revive profits."[7]

The Times went on to say that "the job cuts last month [that] were widespread [were] in transportation, general merchandise, apparel, wholesale trade, publishing, and data processing. The handful of industries that gained ground [that enjoyed increased employment] included retailing, health services, child care and financial services."[8] However, The New York Times apparently found it uncomfortable to tell its readers that most of the industries in which workers were laid off were those that, on average, paid higher wages while most of those that had gained jobs paid on average lower wages.

Workers all over America who did not lose their jobs were also affected by the recession. The Times wrote "wage pressures have subsided. Average hourly earnings for production and non-supervisory workers who hold about 75 percent of the 132 million jobs in April rose by a modest 5 cents to $14.22."[9]

Nothing showed more clearly the inherent conflict of interest between working people and the owners of large number of corporate shares] than an article in the New York Times headed: "More Bad News, And The Stock Market Is **Happy** To Hear It"! As stated in the article, "investors learned to love, or at least to live with, bad news." Why **happy**? Because, "the Dow Jones Industrial Average closed up 154.59 points...near its high for the year...reached on February 1st. The Nasdaq composite index rose 45.53 points."[10]

For instance, regarding layoffs at Dell Corporation, Time Magazine wrote: "Many of the fired workers and their supporters [at Dell Corporation] are attacking the cuts as unnecessary and poorly handled. Some of the workers accuse Dell of targeting older, more <u>highly paid workers</u>. Time quoted Chuck Peterson, one of Dell's laid-off workers, as saying that "the people left are not the ones who built the company. We did all the sweat and now they're getting our stock options." Time went on to say that "Dell rigorously evaluates its employees, ranking each on a descending 1-to-5 scale; fives get fired first. But performance didn't seem to matter this time." Time quoted Gary Davidson as saying that "the first guy in my department to go was the second highest rated on the team."[11]

"In theory," Time wrote, "the fired Dell workers should land on their feet. Most have highly remarkable skills... Every day, they troop to 'a career' center in northwest Austin. They check out websites like computerjobs.com and a bulletin board that boasts 30 'success stories'." Nevertheless as Time pointed out, this is "only limited consolation given that [the] companies where they might naturally land – Intel, Motorola and Verizon – have also been trimming workers." Time quoted 41-year-old Doug Hutter, another laid off Dell employee and a father of two children, as saying, "I'm starting to get scared, I'm wondering where the next house payment is coming from."[12]

None of this worried the owners of Dell's stock which rose 9 percent the day Dell announced it was cutting 1,700 full time jobs.[13]

Although some people may have been happy with the recession, one wonders what thoughts engaged the minds of the other 1,499 workers laid off by Dell. One also wonders what were the feelings of the hundreds of thousands of other workers laid off in the recession of the year 2001.

The recession-depression of the years 2001-2003 was just the latest of the crises that have rocked the business-dominated economic system in the U.S. (see figure 1) Some of these crises have been mild, but others have been severe and thus have had grave consequences for working people and their families.

The Great Depression of the 1930s and Its Consequences for Working People

The greatest ever damage inflicted on the working class was the Great Depression which lasted all through the 1930s. "By 1933, there were anywhere from 12,000,000 to 17,000,000 unemployed. Wage cuts [for those not unemployed] came one after another until they averaged 45% for all industry. Gross farm income dropped from $12 billion to a little over $5 billion."[14] Behind these numbers lay millions of broken lives, broken families and massive social conflict and disruption.

Some of the following descriptions barely scratch the surface of what many felt was abysmal misery.

"As the Depression deepened and destitution increased in the early 1930s, a 'fathomless pessimism' spread across the country. Suicides were common, especially among middle class men who could no longer support their families. Many left their home communities in search of jobs or simply a better life. Estimates of the homeless transients ranged from five hundred thousand to five million. The transients included men as well as women and families. People slept in cars and in parks. Demonstrations and protests intensified. Food riots and hunger riots became more common as crowds of people stormed stores and took the food they needed. Police violence against the demonstrators increased. In March 1932, police attacked a hunger march at the Ford plant in Michigan, killing three marchers and injuring fifty more. In June 1932, some twenty thousand World War I veterans who went to Washington, D.C. accompanied by many women and children to demand early payment of their promised veterans' bonuses were attacked by federal troops who set fire to their encampment.[15]

"As early as the spring of 1930, small and weak companies began to cut wages and to dismiss employees. By November

1930, estimates of unemployment ran between 2,900,000 and 6,900,000. The next year, the situation grew worse. Ever increasing numbers of smaller companies cut wages and their labor forces. By November 1932, the number of unemployed was estimated to run between 11 million and 17 million, with the median figure of around 13.5 million, a total which amounted to roughly one third of the nation's wage earners. In addition large numbers of those not counted as unemployed were working only part time at lower wages.

"Thousands of laborers lost their homes because they could not meet their mortgage payments or pay rent. They built shacks made of scrap metal and egg crates on city dumps. In the cities, bread and soup lines spread endlessly. Many a family literally lived on bread and coffee, some on what they could scavenge from garbage cans. In 1932, there were more than two million 'on the road,' living by theft and beggary."[16]

Louis V. Armstrong, writing of Chicago in 1932, wrote, "One vivid, gruesome moment of those dark days we shall never forget. We saw a crowd of some fifty men fighting over a barrel of garbage which had been set outside the back door of a restaurant. American citizens fighting for scraps of food like animals. Farmers...blockaded roads, overturned milk trucks and sponsored 'shotgun auctions' on farms which had been taken over by foreclosure."[17]

In the winter of 1930-31, a reporter of the time wrote, "You can ride across the lovely Michigan Avenue Bridge [in Chicago] at midnight with the...lights all about making a dream city of incomparable beauty, while twenty feet below you, on the lower level of the same bridge, are 2,000 homeless, decrepit, shivering and starving men, wrapping themselves in old newspapers to keep from freezing and lying down in the manure dust to sleep."[18]

Who can imagine the anguish, the unimaginable suffering, the weeping and sobbing of the thousands and hundreds of thousands of women and children whose husbands abandoned them for not being able to support their families?[19]

The descriptions and scenes depicted here are just the faintest glimpse of the profoundly terrifying and massive distress brought about by the utter failure of the system of "individual enterprise."[20]

"No one knew how to get the wheels [of the economy] going," wrote Lewis Mumford. "Those who knew least as a class were the bankers, the businessmen, the industrialists whose rapacity and inordinate ambitions had largely brought on the catastrophe."[21]

Another severe crisis occurred during the early 1980s and was engineered by the administration of President Reagan. During the Reagan recession, blue collar workers, especially those in the rust belt, suffered the worst job layoffs since 1929. In December 1982, almost 11 million workers were jobless.[22]

Another recession began on July 1990 and ended in 1993. Although during that crisis, at some point in 1991 unemployment averaged only 6.7 percent, an estimated 25 million Americans, or twenty percent of the work force, was jobless. Among the millions was William A. Sullivan, a 52-year-old, who described himself as an independent international business consult. He was found standing with his furniture, Oriental carpets, china and books filling the sidewalk outside the home which he rented for $2,500 a month but was no longer able to afford.[23]

Newsweek, which reported Sullivan's eviction, added, "All over the country business school graduates are telling themselves that if they lose their fancy banking jobs, they can always become consultants in international business. If those guys can't make their rent, what hope is there for the rest of us?"[24]

Just as severely impacted were the workers holding the 20,000 jobs that IBM planned to cut and those who held the more than 70,000 jobs that General motors planned to cut permanently, with no hope of being rehired because GM planned to shut down those plants for good.

The banking industry planned to eliminate 100,000 jobs in 1992. "Manhattan is full of 40 year olds out of work, deep in debt and overextended on their apartments. That's 100,000 middle class people who thought it would never happen to them."[25]

KPMG Peat Marwick, one of the nation's largest accounting firms, dismissed 260 partners in 1991, explaining that "different skills will be needed from now on."

Lee Sliwinski exemplified the human face of job loss. The 50-year-old factory worker drove a forklift for twenty years at the Firestone wheel rim factory south of Detroit. During the 1982 recession, he was earning $10.50 an hour, a pretty good wage for those times, when Firestone laid him off along with 600 other workers. Since then, Sliwinski has gone on welfare twice, lost another factory job in the auto industry and finally, about four years ago, in 1988, landed a job as a janitor, which paid less than $8.50 an hour. Then in 1991, he lost that job as well.[26]

What was new in the recession of the early 1990s was that 85% of those who lost their jobs were "displaced workers." That means that their jobs were gone forever. The Bureau of Labor Statistics (BLS) reported that during the five year period 1987-1991, about 5.6 million workers over the age of twenty permanently lost jobs which they had held for at least three years.[27] The Economic Policy Institute's Lawrence Mishel estimated that if lost permanent jobs held less than three years were added to the Bureau's 1987-1991 count, that total would add up to a whopping 12.3 million jobs.

Whereas in the first year of other recent recessions about 50% of the manufacturing job losses were permanent, during the 1990-1992 recession period, about 85% were. Workers in non-manufacturing jobs suffered equally devastating permanent job losses. Roughly 85% of those who had lost their jobs had no hope of being rehired.[28]

What can be done to eliminate mass unemployment will be discussed in Chapter 15. An account will be given of the ways the capitalist class manages the economy to benefit its interests, and then solutions for a full employment economy will be proposed.

Chapter Fourteen

The Outrageous Consequences of Mass Unemployment

What happens when people lose their jobs and cannot find another for a long time, or when people lose hope of ever finding a job, or start out their adult lives believing they could never earn any kind of living other than in the underground economy, such as selling drugs?

When people have no jobs or lose their jobs for a prolonged period of time they lose control of the most important part of their lives. Not only do the jobless lose the income necessary to maintain a decent material life, their creative impulses are stifled as well. Many of the unemployed channel their energies instead into a variety of antisocial behavior much of which is directed at members of their own families, at people in their own communities or at total strangers. When millions of working people find themselves without jobs, the consequences for all Americans are appalling but for many of America's working people those consequences can be and are frequently dreadful.

What we need to keep in mind as we continue reading the rest of this chapter is the question: If every person capable of working and needing a job and is paid a living wage, would there be all the following outrageous consequences?

One outrageous outcome arising from deliberately created mass unemployment is the costs being paid by the hundreds of thousands of people whose lives are wasted in prison when they could have been of great use to society. For it does not take too great a stretch of the imagination to assume that the overwhelming number of those in prison could not, for a variety of reasons, find jobs. But even if those of us not in prison do not see or do not suffer the agony of those who are in it, we still bear the cost of maintaining those prisons, the prisoners and all their related family problems with our tax dollars, both state and federal.

The Extent of Incarceration

At the end of 2004, there were 2,135,901 persons in local jails, state and federal prisons and juvenile detention centers. "The total adult population under correctional control exceeds 6.6 million. In 2001, the prison population accounted for only 20 percent of the total compared to 60 percent for probationary control, 11 percent for jails and 9 percent for parole".[1]

In 1994, over 90 percent of the inmates were men.. The great majority were poor. The New York Criminal Justice Alliance reported that the typical prison inmate is a young, poorly-educated male who was **unemployed** at the time of arrest.[2] The breakdown on incarceration rates by race, ethnicity and gender in the U.S. in the year 1996 shows that out of every 100,000 residents, 3,098 African-American men were imprisoned, 1,278 Hispanic men and only 370 white men, 88 African-American woman, 78 Hispanic women and only 23 white women. For the 25 to 29 age group men, 10.4 percent of all African-American men or 442,300 persons were in prison. By comparison 2.4 percent of Hispanic men and 1.2 percent of white men in the same age group were in prison. According to the Bureau of Justice statistics, poor African-American males have a 75 percent prospect of going to prison.[3] By the year 2003, whereas minorities accounted for 25 percent of the population, they were 65 percent of the inmate population.

Why, since the 1980s, have so many more minorities than Whites been incarcerated? A law enacted in 1986 imposed 29 new mandatory minimum sentences among which were "notoriously racist disparities in the penalties for crack and powder cocaine Between 1980 and 1990, the number of African Americans who were 12 percent of the population arrested for narcotic charges almost doubled – from 23 percent to 40 percent. In 1985, 800,000 people were arrested on drug charges. By 1989, that number increased to 1.4 million."[4] Some, who knows how many, are likely to resort to drugs to alleviate the pain of joblessness or to sell drugs for a living. It is no surprise therefore that many members of the minorities population are in prison.

Prison populations increase when unemployment rates rise. In 1931, for example, when unemployment was 15.9 percent, as many as 52 persons out of 100,000 were in prison. On the other hand, in 1944 with the unemployment rate at 1.2 percent, 28.4 persons out of 100,000 were in prison. From that low point of 1.2 percent unemployment in 1944, unemployment increased continuously except for brief periods during the Vietnam and Korean wars.[5]

An important cause of the great increase in the prison population since the 1970s was the great reduction of jobs in the manufacturing sector. Since the Second World War, that sector had employed many African-Americans. But when, in the 1970s, hundreds of thousands of jobs were either eliminated or shifted overseas or to Mexico, African-Americans were the hardest hit by unemployment.[6]

A study by the Department of Labor estimated that between 1980 and 1985 "some 2.3 million manufacturing jobs disappeared for good. And as industrial jobs evaporated, so did retail jobs, the local tax base, and much municipal employment."

What is one to do when one loses a job or cannot find one for a lengthy period and perhaps has a family to support? How is one supposed to cope, to survive? Without jobs, some of the jobless will try to survive by mugging, by petty thievery, by robbery, etc. A conservative think-tank reported that one in every three households in the U.S. is touched by major crime in any year.[7] Such are only some of the consequences of mass unemployment.

The monetary costs of mass imprisonment are staggering and they affect most Americans. "Between 1982 and 1997, expenditures on the [entire] correctional [system] increased a whopping 381 percent, police costs jumped 204 percent, and expenses for judicial functions expanded by 267 percent. Total direct spending on the criminal justice system in the U.S. for the 1982-1997 period rose by 262 percent and in 1997 alone approached $130 billion."[8]

Who Gains from the Escalating Imprisonment

Even though most Americans pay heavily for increasing prison population, there are some who actually find it lucrative.

"There are some pretty clear beneficiaries of the prison boom...Smith Barney, Merrill Lynch and other brokerage houses now compete to underwrite prison construction with private tax-exempt bonds. Another securities firm gives its highest recommendation to Correctional Corporation of America [a private corporation], whose directors and executives, reports the Wall Street Journal, include 'certified rainmakers of both political parties'."...Prison construction amounts to a pork barrel for Republicans. Prisons are almost universally built in rural Republican districts, bringing in jobs and dollars...Prison expansion also strengthens the [political] right through its reinforcement of racism…"[9]

If every person needing a job and able to work would be employed and paid a living wage, would we need such a vast network of prisons and prison guards, the entire judicial system, policemen, security guards, etc.? If the over two million persons now in prison had jobs with decent wages, the federal and state taxes they would pay would allow for more social services now being cut in many areas. And it would prevent a host of other staggering personal and social costs.

Widespread Crime as a Consequence of Mass Unemployment

There were 23 million victims of crime during the year 2002. Violent crimes such as rapes, robberies and assaults affected 23 of every 1,000 U.S. residents 12 years and older. For the year 2001, 25 out of every 1,000 U.S. residents were so victimized, 159 persons out of every 1,000 were victims of car theft and burglary. One can only guess how many of theses crimes were committed by the jobless as no attempt has ever been made by any job agency to find out if the perpetrators were jobless at the time of the crime. Would there be as much crime if all able to work and needing a job had one with a living wage?[10]

Stolen Vehicles

If every person able to work and needing a job would have one with a living wage, would so many vehicles be stolen? During the year 1990 for instance, 51,386 cars were stolen in 17 major cities. Thieves have been known to damage parked or passing cars and have even killed pedestrians. Police cars have also been smashed in their attempts to stop the thieves. The victims of the stolen cars are often left stranded and anguished by towing and repair costs.[11]

Muggings

If every person able to work and needing a job would have one with a living wage, would there be as many muggings and related killings? Muggings are perpetrated by people who waylay and beat severely, usually with intent to rob, but very rarely with intent to kill. Most muggings are not reported and therefore are not part of any official statistics. What has been reported are the muggings of some of our "respectable" citizens, who despite their higher social status are not immune.

The following are just two such instances. George Delacorte, a 92-year-old philanthropist, was robbed in New York's Central Park. The two robbers, seventeen and twenty years old, stole $200 in cash from Mr. Delacorte, and a valuable mink coat from his wife. They then tried to choke his wife and stabbed her right hand.

Another case involving an attorney ended in tragedy. While strolling at sunset through an isolated section of East River Park in lower Manhattan, Patrick Kehn and his companion, Mary Murphy, were robbed by three youths. After handing over all their cash and Miss Murphy's gold neck chain and wrist watch, Mr. Kehn was beaten with a baseball bat and was stabbed with a hunting knife in his chest and abdomen. Mr. Kehn's murder was only one of a record 1,826 homicides in New York in 1980, a 63 percent increase from 1970.[12]

Also tragic was the robbery and murder of Gail F. Shollar, a 35-year-old mother of a 10-year-old daughter, an 8-year-old son and a 3 and a half-year-old daughter. On a routine shopping trip, she was slain by 23 year old Scott Johnson, who robbed Mrs. Shollar of $1.90. According to his estranged wife, he was distraught because he lost his job and needed money to pay child support. Mr. Shollar, now widowed with 3 children, dragged himself out of his wife's funeral "limp and sobbing."[13]

Rampage Killings

The mass murders of people, many of them total strangers to the murderers, are another of the many costs innocent people in the larger community pay for the many jobless. The tragedy of 5 dead and 20 wounded on a Long Island train on Dec. 7, 1993 is just one of many such rampage killings. The murderer, Colin Ferguson, was **unemployed**. Rampage killings began in 1966 when sniper Charles Whitman killed 16 people. In 1984, James Oliver Huberty killed 20, 5 of them children and wounded 16 more, one mortally, at a McDonald's fast food store in San Isidro, California. Was he jobless? The report in McCalls did not say. But if he was fully employed with a living wage, would he be likely to inflict such horror on others?

On Dec. 2, 1993, Alan Winterbourne, a jobless adult killed three and wounded four at an unemployment office in Oxnard, California and then also killed the police officer who pursued him. In 1989, five children were shot dead by Patrick Purdy in a Stockton, California, schoolyard. In 1990, nine people were killed by James Edward Pough at a General Motors auto financing center in Jacksonville, Florida. In 1991, 23 people were killed by George Hennard in Luby's Cafeteria in Killteen, Texas.

Such multiple murders occur about 30 times a year according to James Fox – dean of the college of Criminal Justice at Northeastern University in Boston.[14] Were all these mass murderers unemployed or only those specifically mentioned as unemployed? Would people working full time with a living wage be likely to commit such horrendous acts?

Some farmers who lost their lands and thus their source of livelihood went on a similar murderous rampage. Dale Burr, a 63-year-old farmer about to lose his land, machinery, stored grains and his beloved quarter-horse, killed John Hughes, president of the Hills Bank and Trust Company. Burr shot two other people to death before committing suicide. In 1983, James Jenkins, a Minnesota farmer, and his son Steve who had lost his land, cattle, and credit rating, lured Rudoph H. Blythe Jr. the local bank president and his loan officer to the abandoned farm and killed them both before Mr. Jenkins shot himself.[15]

In the society such as ours, the cornerstone of any working person's identity and sense of self-esteem depends on a job with a decent income. Being jobless leaves one with a very poor sense of self. In our society where people are generally evaluated on the basis of what they do for a living, a jobless person is almost thought of as an outcast. Sometimes when the loss of a job comes at a time of other severe problems, a person is likely to snap, letting loose destructive impulses.

In 1999, about to be dismissed by Xerox in Hawaii, 40 year old Byron Uyesugi shot and killed seven co-workers at his company's office.[16] In 2003, Salvador Tapia, fired from his warehouse job six months earlier, shot to death six men in the warehouse. Among the victims were two brothers who were owners of the warehouse. Tapia then killed himself. In 1986, Pat Sherrill killed 14 people and wounded 20 others.[17] In 1998, Mark Boston killed nine people at a stock trading firm in Atlanta, after killing his wife and two children. Some tourists also paid the price of joblessness. Nine foreign tourists were slain in Florida during 1992 and 1993.[18]

Who are the rampage killers? A study undertaken by the New York Times found that the most common precipitator – the spark that set off the tinder – was the loss of a job. Job loss was the potential cause in 47 out of the 100 rampage attacks during the last 50 years. The study found that a total of 425 people were killed and 510 injured. These figures include the 1998 Columbine High School shootings which had nothing to do with the loss of jobs.[19]

Inner-City Murders

The most numerous murders – those that receive scant attention – occur in the inner cities. In just one of many examples, there were 1200 murder victims in Florida, wrote a Nation editorial in 1993. Most of the murder victims lived nor far from the white sands of Miami Beach - the same area where the murders of foreign tourists occurred. In that neighborhood, there exists a cauldron of drugs, weapons and despair... mostly the despaired kill one another.[20] The editorial does not spell out the cause of the despair, but could it be joblessness? The Federal Bureau of Investigation reported that in 2004 there were a total of 14,121 victims of murder. Of these, 6,929 were Whites and 6,632 were African Americans. Whereas African Americans make up 13.3 percent of the population, they suffered 47.6 percent of all murder victims. That large number of murders among African Americans has been attributed indirectly to their very high unemployment rate by William Julius Wilson, Chicago University Professor of Sociology in his book The Truly Disadvantaged.

Impact on Families

Families whose breadwinners are laid off without any hope of being recalled suffer stress, depression and demoralization. Such circumstances worsen for some families. One study indicated that such families suffer violent behavior six times greater than do families of the employed. Alcohol abuse is seven times greater.[21]

No consequences of unemployment are as appalling as those that befall women and children. Every year all Americans pay billions of dollars for child welfare services, additional billions to combat domestic violence against women, and billions more for foster care. The number of children affected every year by domestic violence is an astounding four million. In 1994, in California alone, there were 664,000 abused and neglected children, costing the state $652 million in child welfare services.[22] How many more children are abused nationwide and how much is spent on child welfare services by all the states is anybody's guess but they can hardly be insignificant. A 1997 report hints at the numbers. "Like all urban areas, Washington, D. C., is home to a heart-wrenching number of abused and neglected children. From August to October 1996, the city's child abuse and neglect hotline received more than 400 substantiated reports of child abuse and neglect. Some 6,700 children are under the city's supervision."[23]

Every year, fifty percent of women in California will be assaulted by their husbands, ex-husbands or sons. In 1995, California law enforcement agencies made 45,197 felony domestic violence arrests. In 1998, the state total dropped to 40,111 arrests.[24] The FBI estimates that one in three women in the U.S. will be sexually assaulted in her lifetime. Sexual assaults are motivated by anger, hostility and a need to control.[25] The phrase 'need to control' comes up in a number of reports on domestic and other kinds of violence.

People have an inherent need to control the most important part of their lives and that part of their lives is having a job that not only provides a decent income, but also a sense of being a useful part of society from whence they gain much of their self-esteem.

When people lose their jobs or have no hope of finding a job or are jobless for a prolonged period of time, they become angry and tend to want to compensate for the loss of control of the most important part of their lives by a more complete control over others. Family members, being the weakest and nearest, bear the brunt. How many of the abusers of women and children are victims of jobless men is hard to know. No government or any other agency has ever tried to find out if the abusers were jobless. Would so much abuse occur if everyone needing a job would have one that would provide a living wage?

Reaction to unemployment varies from one income group to another. Low-income people burdened with serious family problems and who live from one paycheck to another are more likely to react with greater anger and hostility and even violence towards those around them.

Here are a few such instances. Kevin Shannon, a 42-year-old unemployed San Franciscan, killed his ten-year-old son, Grant and them himself in front of his wife.[26]

A 47-year-old San Jose man, Kam Lun Aloysius Lee, worried about losing his job at a local high tech company, shot his wife and their two children 9-and-4-years old. This was the fifth family murder suicide in Northern California in 2002.[27]

How do working people with a middle income react when they lose their jobs? A study of ten managerial and professional persons who lost their jobs found that two of the ten suffered chronic disabilities. One of these two became permanently disabled and the other became psychologically unable to cope with job rejections and stopped looking for any job. Two wives of their unemployed husbands considered separation and or divorce, while the partner of an unemployed woman began an affair. Though later four of the individuals found good jobs, "all of them expressed high levels of anxiety and uncertainty about their professional future, fearing another job loss. That uncertainly, combined with the stress of adjusting to a new highly demanding position, impacted negatively on the relationship with their spouses or partners and to a lesser degree with their children. The individuals who did not find jobs experienced an ever increasing sense of depression, hopelessness and despair. Some began to overeat or drink more than previously, others withdrew and spent hours watching television, listening to music and using the Internet while still others sought escape outside the home. For the spouse or partner of the employed person, an ever-increasing spiral of anger, resentment and guilt developed.[28]

Other consequences of mass unemployment are increased welfare costs, the costs of housing and caring for the homeless and rising costs of health care for the jobless. All these consequences add severe stresses to the budgets of the Federal and State governments.

Welfare Costs

Every recession with its accompanying higher rates of unemployment swells the amount of money the Federal and State governments have to pay out. To take just one example, the recession of 1991 drove up welfare expenditures for a record 12.4 million people, a million more than the previous peak in 1976; food stamps recipients jumped 10 percent to 21.7 million in a year and the Federal Government expected half a million more for each program in 1992. The need to spend more for a larger number of jobless was also bad news for the states which pay 45 percent of the nation's $20 billion welfare tab. "Already strapped, they [the States] must cough up more than $5 billion in extra unanticipated spending.[29]

Homelessness

In New York City, just emerging from the recession [of 2001-2003], there were more homeless people than at any time ... since the 1970s... A survey of 25 American cities showed an increase of 17 percent in requests for emergency food assistance and an increase of 13% in requests for emergency shelter.[30]

Washington, D.C., has a homeless population of 5,000 to 15,000 people. Sheltering all of them would cost the city $60 million and bankrupt the local budget. In New York alone, expenditures for the homeless swelled from $15 million to $200 million in five years since 1980.[31]

Health Costs

When people become jobless for a long period of time, it could result in poverty and ill health. It is no wonder then that a large number of jobless people who have become sick have to resort to Medicaid, the cost of which is spiraling.

Arsons, Bank Robberies and Shoplifting

Timothy Ingalsbee, director of the Fire Ecology Center in Eugene, Oregon, estimated that about one-quarter of all fires – more than 25,000 fires – are caused by arson and another 25,000 might be. One wonders: How many of those fires were started by persons who were either unemployed or only part time employed and were angry enough to resort to arson in the hope of not being caught? In 2002, Leonard Greg, a 29 year old part-time fire-fighter set fire to dry grass in the hope of earning $8 an hour as a full-time fire-fighter. The fire set by Gregg caused economic devastation across an area famous for hunting, fishing and scenic beauty. Show Low and other communities north of Cibecue, Arizona, mostly populated by Whites, lost more than 420 homes. The Apache lost pine forests that supported a timber industry employing hundreds of tribe members. Such are the dreadful consequences of just one person needing a full-time job but had only a part-time job.[32]

Richard Mangan, a retired Forest Service Fire Administrator in Missoula, Montana, estimated that as many as twenty wild fires a year are deliberately started by fire-fighters. Ingalsbee said, "Federal policy changes over the past generation have privatized the fire-fighting support network – the water tankers, planes, food and other services used by crews nationwide, thus creating fire entrepreneurs whose livelihood depends on flame." Can one imagine such entrepreneurs sitting idle and not tempted to make a profit? Such fires destroy the homes and everything in them of completely innocent people. Who can imagine the extent of their anguish?[33]

Bank Robberies and Killings

In Northern California alone and in just one year, 2001-2002, there were 90 take-over robberies. During the previous year there were 70 such robberies. From 1997 to 2002, there were a total of 2,305 bank robberies in the 15 counties from Monterey to Del Norte Counties.

Though banks are the victims, they most likely compensate themselves by raising the fees they charge us, their customers. But some people pay the ultimate price. One armored-car guard, 20-year-old Thomas Wheelock, shot to death his partner Rodrigo Cortez before taking off with $300,000. Wheelock was worried about losing his job.[34]

Dena Monique Daniels, a Brinks Inc. guard, was killed by two masked men in Berkeley, California. A month earlier a Wells

Fargo bank manager, 34-year-old Alice Martel of Millbrae, California, was killed by bank robbers. Ms. Martel had two sons ages 2 and 4 who are now being raised by her husband, David.

It is, of course, difficult to know how many of the people who commit bank robberies are unemployed or despaired of ever landing a full-time job with a living wage. But again, one may wonder if any person would risk long prison sentences or even the death penalty were they offered legitimate alternatives.

Shoplifting

Another of the consequences of unemployment is the mass shoplifting from retail stores. A survey of 3,500 retailers showed losses of $1.9 billion in California alone, noted Julia Bell, attorney for Sears. She added that shoplifting arrests climbed 19% from 1974 to 1979. That turns out, she said, to $200 a year per customer.[35] Retailers have been known to add a certain percentage to the cost of their goods to compensate themselves for losses due to shoplifting. Guess who pays?

Social Costs of Low Wage Employment

People earning low wages rather than a living wage has its own ugly consequences for society. Jeffrey Grogger, a fellow at the respected National Bureau of Economic Research, found that the more money young men make through legitimate jobs, the less likely they are to commit crimes. His study found that a 10% increase in wages would reduce youth participation in crime by roughly 6-9%. His calculations found that, conversely, a 20% wage drop leads to a 12-18% increase in youth participation in crime. Grogger found that since the 1970s, hourly wages for 16-to 24-year-old males had fallen by 23%. Federal Bureau of Investigation data show that from the early 1970s to the late 1980s, arrest rates for young males rose from 44.6 per thousand to 52.6 per thousand, an increase of 18 percent.[36]

Unrest and Destructive Riots

When the destructive riots with their murderous rage and destruction during the last five decades broke out, the common spark that set them off was in most cases the killings of African-Americans by police. Most official reports of those events made no mention of the fact that the rioters were mostly young men and women who had endured long periods of joblessness or had no hope of finding a legitimate job.

The riots in Cincinnati in April of 2001 broke out after the city's police killed thirteen African-Americans from 1995-2000 and the latest killing was the fourth African American since November 2000. Dozens of the city's stores were damaged. Defenders of the police actions complained that African-Americans kill most of the police slain in the line of duty.[37]

Working people who live in areas with poor schools, inferior living conditions and **high rates of unemployment** will react violently whenever they endure acts of police brutality or other kinds of violence threatening their self-esteem. Since the 1960s, this volatile mixture has exploded in three large scale riots that have resulted in massive destruction of property, the killings of numerous rioters and injury to many officers.

Sparked by the assassination of Martin Luther King Junior, the 1965 riots in the Watts neighborhood of Los Angeles accounted for 34 rioters killed and 1,032 injured. Among the injured were 90 Los Angeles police officers, 136 firemen, 10 National Guardsmen, 23 from government agencies and 773 civilians. Property damage amounted to over $40 million and

more than six hundred buildings were damaged by either burn-
ing or looting; Two hundred buildings were destroyed by fire.

In 1970, in East Los Angeles, another riot erupted, this time
after the police attempted to disperse a crowd of some 20,000
Mexican Americans who were protesting peacefully against the
Vietnam War. The damage to property amounted to $1 million,
while 3 people were killed and 60 injured. The organizers of the
protest argued that a degrading welfare system plus **a lack of
job opportunities** pushed young Mexican-American men toward military service.[38]

In 1992, when the four Los Angeles police officers who had
brutally beaten African American Rodney King were acquitted
by a mostly white jury, hell broke loose in that city. The material
damage from the riots has been estimated at between $800
million and $1 billion. About 3,600 fires were set which de-
stroyed 1,100 buildings. About 10,000 people were arrested of
whom 42% were African Americans, 44% Latinos and 9% white.
Much of the looting was done by young men – African Americans, Hispanics and Whites. Smaller riots occurred in Las Vegas,
Atlanta, San Francisco, Oakland, New York, Seattle, Chicago,
Phoenix, and Madison, WI. The South Central neighborhood
of Los Angeles, where the rioters lived, had **"extremely high
unemployment among its residents."**[39]

Impact of Mass Unemployment on Law Enforcement Officers

The group that bears the greatest burden and pays the
highest price for mass unemployment is the country's police
officers. In his welcoming remarks at the 2002 Candlelight Vigil
in memory of the many police officers fallen in the line of duty,
Craig W. Floyd told his audience that from 1872 to 2002, a total
of 16,000 officers had fallen in the line of duty and that in 2001,

230 officers were killed, the most since 1974. He said that each year, an average of 61,000 officers are assaulted, 19,000 injured and one killed every 53 hours.[40]

Pervasive Feelings of Insecurity

If every person able to work and needing a job would have one with a living wage, would we all feel as insecure as we do in our homes, businesses and in other public places? The fear of crime is so pervasive that we spend vast amounts of money and other resources to secure our personal safety, our houses, our homes and our properties. Businesses as well as various levels of government have felt compelled to spend lots of money to secure their premises.

Go to any of the malls and other large shopping centers and one cannot avoid the presence of security guards. Who pays their wages? Most likely their wages are paid indirectly by the many store owners who rent space in these malls and shopping centers and who then add that expense to the price of their goods and services. In the end, it is the people who buy those goods and services who pay the wages of the security guards. The same my be said for security guards in all the hotels, private offices, government buildings and just about every place that hires them. In fact employment has been growing faster in the security industry than in any other.

Our fear of crime compels us to install security systems in our homes and cars to prevent vandalism and theft. The total cost amounts to billions of dollars. For low-income car and home owners struggling to make ends meet, the financial burden of such costs can hardly be light. And who pays for the electronic and other kinds of security devices protecting the gated communities of the well-to-do?

The White House and Congress used to be free of fences and security guards.

Now both institutions are protected by concrete blocks, fences and scores of security personnel. Who pays? Could it be our taxes which never cease to rise?

The public's fear of crime has also prompted our political leaders to advocate for the recruitment of more police officers. Remember when President Clinton called for an additional 100,000 police officers. Who pays if not our taxes?

Low income people living in or near the inner cities of our great metropolitan centers are at the greatest risk of crime, especially break-ins from the unemployed. Such people make incredible efforts to provide security for their homes. Insecurity has compelled one such neighborhood to adopt extreme measures. In a section of the Bronx in New York, one retired home owner fenced himself behind window gratings and wrought-iron gates backed by wire mesh and topped by gleaming coils of razor ribbons. Over the last decade, razor ribbon has spread from stores and other businesses to homes, libraries, churches and drug rehabilitation centers.[41]

How Mass Unemployment Weakens the Bargaining Power of Workers

The closing of numerous factories employing millions of well-paid workers has reduced the membership of many industrial unions. This has also reduced the membership dues paid to the unions. From a peak 35 percent of the total work force in the 1940s, union membership has dwindled to 14.5 percent in 1996. With fewer financial resources, the ability of workers' unions to compete with the owning class in electoral politics has greatly diminished. When many millions are unemployed, it chills the willingness of the employed to vote for a strike for fear that they would be replaced by scabs. Because employers are free to replace striking workers with scabs, workers tend to accept lower wages and benefits rather than walk out of their jobs. Thus, whereas in the peak strike year of 1974, there were 424 strikes involving 1,000 workers or more, in 1996 there were only 37 such strikes.[42]

When many young White men, with no more than a high school education or less, have a difficult time finding jobs, many of them tend to blame other ethnic or racial groups or immigrants or even the Federal government. Young White men, if they did find a job, earned 30 percent less in 1989 than they did 10 years ago.[43] Much unemployment, which has resulted by the closing of military basis, the bankruptcy of numerous family farms, and the elimination of millions of well-paid blue collar jobs, have created a large number of Americans having great difficulty in making ends meet. The consequence has been the rise and growth of militia and Patriot organizations.

"Since 1995, the number of militia and Patriot organizations has increased 6% to 858 identifiable groups, including 380 armed ones. Terry Nichols, indicted for helping to plan the Oklahoma City bombing, started his Patriot career by becoming involved in groups that helped farmers hold on to their land by fighting the government and banks. Arthur Hawkins, a 40-year-old father of six, joined a series of anti-government groups after he lost his job as a corrections officer in Kansas. Bob Fletcher became a spokesman for the militia of Montana, and then a talk radio host after his Georgia-based toy company went bankrupt.[44]

The Huge Monetary Costs and Job Losses

Mass unemployment's most outrageous and huge costs to all Americans are the loss over the last 75 years of many trillions of dollars worth of goods and services that would have been produced if we had full employment. It has been estimated that just between 1953 and 1979 we have forfeited $7.1 trillion in Gross National Product and 80.8 million years of civilian employment opportunities and consequently lost about $1.8 trillion in public revenue at all levels [alongside] severe neglect of national priorities and chronically rising Federal budget deficits. In addition, the empirical evidence for more than a quarter of a century [1953-1978] has demonstrated that inflation rises as unused capabilities [unemployed human labor and idle machines] increase.[45]

If we had full employment during 1953-1979, $1.8 trillion in taxes could have been collected. The $260 billion in total federal deficits during this period could have been avoided and the huge balance could have been used to serve well rather than seriously under-serve the great domestic national priorities.[46]

Chapter Fifteen

Solutions to the Problem of Mass Unemployment

What Does Full Employment Mean?

Full employment would require the number of job openings be equal to the number of those willing and able to work. An even better full employment would mean the number of jobs be greater than the number of job seekers. This would give working people a choice among available jobs rather than giving employers a choice among available workers. Why not a Department of Full Employment in the Federal Government that would conduct a periodical survey of job needs? Why not a jobs bank? For, as we have seen in Chapter 6, when there is an abundance of jobless workers, it is the employer who has the advantage when bargaining with a prospective employee. Conversely, when there are more jobs than willing workers, the bargaining power of workers both individually and collectively increases. This would enhance the welfare and the dignity of working people. What a wonderfully positive contribution that could make to America's general welfare!

And as have shown in Chapters 7-11, the drive for maximum profits compels employers to reduce the cost of labor in the U.S. They seek cheap labor wherever in the world it can be found. They replace workers with a never-ending introduction of advanced technology. They acquire or merge companies so as to eliminate jobs and they import cheap labor to replace domestic workers. Chapter 12 provided a brief account about how and why the Federal Reserve keeps unemployment at a high level.

If therefore the way our economic system is presently organized cannot ever create a society of full employment, what can be done to create it? This chapter will first lay out the badly needed programs that will create the abundance of needed jobs. These programs will benefit all Americans. Full employment will provide working people with a lot more money to buy a far greater amount of goods and services than they can afford at present. Full employment will also eliminate most if not all the very costly and outrageous consequences of mass unemployment. We will then outline the sources from which those programs can be funded. Finally, we will discuss the political feasibility of the proposed solutions.

The Programs that will Create Jobs

Housing

The most acute need is for a massive federally funded program to build decent low-cost housing and make it available to the many millions of working people and, especially, to the homeless, who are now desperately in need of permanent and minimally decent shelter. "Nearly 6 in 10 working poor families lack decent, affordable rental housing and many of these households include full-time minimum wage earners. Children reside in 60% of these families who are often forced to choose between basic necessities and paying the rent."[1]

Old and rundown housing needs to be torn down and rebuilt and many new housing complexes need to be built and planned so as to provide all the needed services within walking distance. This will eliminate the burden for many working families of buying and maintaining vehicles. Especially urgent is the need to build sturdy concrete housing in tornado-and hurricane-prone areas to replace homes built of wood.

Mass Transit

A vast network of buses and trains is badly needed. At present, such services as we have are ridiculously inadequate and inefficient. For example, Amtrak, our national train service, runs at a maximum speed of 70 miles per hour and is beset by problems, not the least of which are recurrent accidents involving fatalities.

A country as vast as ours would greatly benefit from a high-speed magnetic rail system, with trains that travel at 250 miles an hour. Many existing idle American factories and unemployed workers could be used to produce trains similar to those built in Japan and Europe. Is it not amazing that South Korea, a country far smaller than the U.S. and with far fewer resources, has trains that travel at speeds up to 185 miles per hour? Taiwan is inaugurating a similar train, and China will soon build one to connect its capital, Beijing, with Shanghai. If Japan, France, Germany and Spain all have such high-speed trains, why doesn't the U.S. the wealthiest nation, have them? It is because if working people would use high-speed trains instead of their vehicles, it would cause catastrophic losses both in wealth and power for the owners of the automobile and gas corporations. And they have therefore used their wealth and power in Congress to prevent any kind of meaningful funding for the development of high-speed trains.

Not only would high-speed trains avoid the terrible and nerve-wracking congestion and delays caused by traffic accidents on the freeways, it would save long distance commuters much needed funds presently used for gas, automobile license fees, insurance coverage and maintenance. It would have the added benefit of eliminating much of our dependence on oil, which is responsible for the destruction of the lives of many of our young men and women and the squandering of billions of dollars on military adventures in the Middle East and elsewhere.

Overhauling and Expanding the Nation's Infrastructure

Many of our roads, bridges and sewer systems having been built decades ago need to be replaced. New infrastructure is needed for our central cities and other rundown urban centers such as Camden, New Jersey, and East St. Louis, Illinois. "And there is plenty of [other] work to be done. For instance, the American Society of Civil Engineers recently found that U. S. infrastructure needs over $1.3 trillion in new spending over the next five years, simply to reach what it calls acceptable standards. That includes much needed improvements in schools, sewers, airports, mass transit systems, roads and other vital infrastructures..."[2]

Education

Much work needs to be done to improve the education of our youth. Most urgently needed are far more vocational programs than are presently available for our youth, now adrift. The aptitudes of these many of these young might be suitable for jobs such as carpenters, electricians, plumbers, auto mechanics, machinists, etc. – skills that will be in great demand once the vast construction works outlined here are undertaken.

Many more teachers are needed so that many presently overcrowded classes can be reduced to fewer students to make both teaching and learning more rewarding. Teachers need to be free of a rigid curriculum that limits them to raising SAT scores. They also need to be free to provide instruction in the ability to reason and in critical analysis, abilities presently sorely lacking in many of our public schools. Many schools need to be built and others repaired and renovated. Similar overhaul is likely to be needed for many buildings on college and university campuses.

Energy

A vast program for renewable sources of energy should be put in place. Private homes, public buildings and corporations could save billions of dollars in electric and natural gas bills if they could harness the sun's energy by laying out photovoltaic panels on their roofs. Energy companies, either private or government-owned, could use wind and water power to generate much of the energy now generated by coal and oil, which are polluting the environment.

Health Care

Badly needed is a complete overhaul of our health care system. While many millions of people – some 38 million as of 1992 – are without any health insurance and thus suffer from treatable diseases, many hospitals have been closed. Many corporations have recently been reducing health coverage for their employees at the very time when the costs of health care coverage are soaring. Many workers still employed thus fear that if they change jobs or are fired, they will lose all medical coverage. The cost of health care has risen ten times since 1950.

This huge increase is supposedly due to the introduction of high tech medical equipment. We are not told that most of this increase is due to the unbridled profiteering by health insurance companies and HMOs, and medical forms-processing bureaucracies. Needed on a vast scale, which would produce hundreds of thousands of jobs, are hospitals and clinics especially in areas of severe unemployment. Such facilities are scarce in areas where citizens lack health insurance, yet have the highest incidence of curable ailments.

Recently Medicaid, which serves the minimal needs of the poor and Medicare, which insures the elderly, have both been under assault by the second Bush administration. Also the pharmaceutical companies are riding roughshod on consumers by charging us the highest drug prices in the world. It has been reported that veterans' health needs are also being short-changed. What if we were to adopt a single-payer national health care system which would guarantee health care for all Americans? Such a system, funded by our tax dollars, would cost much less than the present fragmented system and would be less burdensome for all and would even free up resources for the construction of new health care facilities.

Environment

A gigantic task requiring the labor of brigades of workers will be the cleaning up the environment. That includes our rivers, lakes and aquifers, the reclaiming of lands ravaged by mining, quarrying, overuse, and erosion. Many areas need reforesting and new parks and wildlife refuges need to be built. Reforestation will provide a renewable source of energy.

Child Care

The lack of adequate and decent childcare centers is one of our most acute social problems. Our society cannot have it both ways. If women work because men do not earn enough to support their families, what is sorely needed is a widespread network of excellent childcare facilities and well-trained and well-paid personnel to staff them. This would not only produce a very large number of jobs but would also provide all of our children with a good overall start in life.

Teen Recreational Centers

The need for building and staffing decent and attractive recreational facilities all over the country for teenagers is another badly needed resource. These centers should be open until midnight for teenagers bursting with energy. When nothing recreational and good character-building activities are offered to teenagers after school, they will gravitate to any kind of activity that will absorb their energies. Good teen recreational centers would eliminate much of the juvenile delinquency so rampant in many of the communities where parents cannot afford to pay for any kind of extracurricular activities. If the collective villages of Israel with their meager resources can afford to have just such centers, then surely the world's wealthiest country can afford them and do even better.

Parks

Cities and towns with many newly built, large, green-filled parks would be a much more attractive place of residence for people living in desolate urban areas or in heavily wooded areas prone to terrifying fires during years of drought. Think of how many gardeners and landscapers now either unemployed or only partially employed would be delighted and inspired to work on such projects. And what about city and town dwellers? Not only would such parks allow for some needed community activity but would also absorb much if not all the carbon dioxide vehicles generate.

The Many Benefits of Full Employment

Once full employment with living wages becomes an integral part of the economy, the entire society will gain.

With full employment or more full employment at living wages: The economy will produce more and will thus provide more in revenue for the Federal government, without the need to raise taxes.

1) More individuals will be able to earn a decent living and therefore will not need the help of welfare benefits or transfer payments such as tax credits.
2) More working people will be able to buy much more of the goods produced by farmers. There will then be less need to limit output or to provide federal, state or local subsidies and other support for farm prices.
3) More enterprises will be able to earn profits without the need for monopolies and oligopolies to charge high prices or lobby for government welfare, and consumers will be able to enjoy lower prices.
4) More people will be able to afford adequate housing, thus needing less government subsidy. If every American could be guaranteed decent, safe and sanitary housing—and housing that could also be provided with adequate maintenance and weatherization, and if millions of existing build-

ings were rehabilitated, there would be a need to build new roads, storm sewers, sewage and refuse disposal.

5) More tax revenues would be available to pay for expanded health services for the larger numbers of people both the young and the elderly.

6) More tax revenues could finance social security, Medicare, Medicaid, Workers' Compensation for the injured and welfare for the physically and mentally impaired. More local, state and federal tax revenues would be available to help support education and lifelong learning.

Where is the money to come from for the many job programs?

The money to carry out this vast array of modernizing and renewing activities of both our physical and human needs will have to come from the presently swollen military budgets, from the taxes not being paid by highly profitable corporations, from the tax cuts and other subsidies doled out to the corporations, and from the taxes that will be paid by the jobless millions when they start working.

Lots of money presently exists but they are spent for purposes that serve mostly the interests of a very small part of our population. Much of those billions of dollars are spent on unnecessary weapons and wars and they benefit mainly all those connected with the tightly entwined military industrial financial (MIF) complex.

The Military Industrial Financial (MIF) Complex

This unholy trinity, the MIF, has become nothing less than a cancer, eating away at every healthy part of our society, and now doing so faster than at any earlier time in our history. During the fiscal year 2002, for instance, the resources devoured by the military-industrial-financial interests included not only the $344 billion spent by the Department of Defense but also the interest, which that year alone, amounted to $138 billion and paid largely to wealthy individuals and banks which had lent money to the government for its military spending.

Adding the interest component to all of the other military expenditures of the Departments of Defense, Energy, State, Veterans Affairs and Homeland Security, the 2002 defense budget amounted to $596.1 billion. "We will have every reason to suppose," writes Robert Higgs, that "in fiscal year 2004, the grand total spent for defense will be $695 billion. To this amount will have to be added the $58.8 billion from the 89.5 billion authorized on November 6, 2003. Thus the super-grand total for 2004 "will reach the astonishing amount of nearly $754 billion...plus of course, any additional supplemental spending that may be approved before the end of 2004.

"Therefore," Higgs continues, "I propose that in considering future defense budgetary costs, a well-founded rule of thumb is to take the Pentagon's...basic budget total and double it. You may overstate the truth, but if so, you'll not do so by much."[3]

"By 2009 and thereafter," writes Robert S. McIntyre, Director of Citizens for Tax Justice, "the government is likely to be spending more on interest or the [national] debt than all domestic discretionary programs—from education to environmental protection, to law enforcement, to science, to transportation and to veterans."

To whom are the monies spent on the military going? Although Halliburton is much in the news as making billions in the so-called rebuilding of Iraq, most of the money is being poured into the cash boxes of the three largest weapons makers. They are Lockheed Martin, Boeing and Northrop Grumman.

"In fiscal year 2002," writes William D. Hartung, a senior research fellow at the World Policy Institute at the New School, the Big Three received a total of more than $42 billion in Pentagon contracts, of which Lockheed Martin got $17 billion, Boeing $16.6 billion and Northrop Grumman $8.7 billion. "Lockheed Martin has a $2 billion a year contract to run...a nuclear weapons design and engineering facility...and also works in partnership with Bechtel to run the Nevada [nuclear] test site." Both "Boeing and Lockheed Martin are also poised to profit from Bush's plan to colonize the Moon and send a manned mission to Mars, both of which are stalking horses for launching an arms race to space." The Big Three will also gain from "numerous other sources of federal contracts for everything from airport security to domestic surveillance."[4]

Many former high-ranking officers and officials have questioned the bloated nature of the Military Industrial Financial complex (MIF). As recently as 1999, Paul Nitze, a former arms control negotiator and an ambassador at large in the Reagan administration, wrote that he saw no compelling reason why we should not unilaterally get rid of our nuclear weapons. To maintain them is costly and adds nothing to our security.[5] Why then did George Bush Jr. disregard his advice by continuing the $2 billion a year contract with Lockheed Martin to run a nuclear weapons design and engineering facility?

Seymour Melman, professor of industrial engineering at New York's Columbia University, spelled out the enormously high cost of feeding the voracious appetite of the MIF. From 1949 to 1989, the total budget of the Defense Department (in 1982 dollars), was $8.2 trillion. That was greater than the total monetary value of the nation's entire civilian industrial plants and equipment and of the nation's infrastructure in 1982, a total of $7.3 trillion. In other words, the government has invested more capital [money] for military purposes than would be needed to replace most of the machines and structures that serve the civilian [non-military] sectors of the country.[6]

What happens when such enormous amounts of our taxes – the sweat and blood of our daily labors goes into making nuclear weapons, military airplanes, tanks, etc.? The result, as described by Professor Melman, is that, "the decay in U.S. civilian industry has been proceeding swiftly toward a situation akin to underdevelopment. Consider the disappearance of factories and labor forces from the machine-producing industries of the United States. From 1979 to 1987, 50 percent of production workers disappeared from the machine tool industry, 60 percent from the turbine and turbine generator industry, 42 percent from the construction machinery industry, 43 percent from the textile equipment industry, 68 percent from the gas-field equipment industry." What has in fact occurred is an "avalanche of plant closings in these and other machinery production industries."[7]

The justification for the endlessly wasteful funding of the military has been that it preserves and creates jobs. But any dollar that goes to the MIF would create two to three times as many jobs in projects dedicated to building a high speed train network, projects dedicated to building schools, day care and teen centers as well as maintaining many roads, bridges and schools.[8]

The Threat Posed by the MIF Complex to Our Fragile Democracy

After each war over which they presided, four of our most popular leaders have warned us of the overwhelming power that would accumulate in the hands of the military-industrial complex. And every one of those leaders called us to be alert to the dangers posed by that power.

In his farewell address on September 17, 1796, President George Washington, who presided over America's War of Independence, said "Overgrown military establishments are under any form of government inauspicious to liberty, and are to be regarded as particularly hostile to Republican liberty."[9]

Abraham Lincoln, president during the catastrophic Civil War, having witnessed the rise of corporations in the wake of that war, expressed deep concern: "I see in the future a crisis approaching that unnerves me and causes me to tremble for the safety of my country. As a result of the [Civil] War, corporations have been enthroned and an era of corruption in high places will follow, and the money powers of the country will endeavor to prolong its reign by working upon the prejudices [read fear] of the people, until all the wealth is aggregated in a few hands and the Republic is destroyed."[10]

Before and between the two world wars, Marine Brigadier General Smedley D. Butler, another major figure in America's history, warned of the growing power of the military-industrial-financial complex. General Butler died in 1940 a few months before the attack on Pearl Harbor. In his book, *War Is A Racket*, he wrote how his career as a general enriched some major corporations. Explaining why such corporations tend to be enthusiastic about war, he wrote, "The normal profits of a business concern in the U.S. are six, ten and sometimes even twelve per cent. But wartime profits—ah! That is another matter – twenty, sixty, one hundred three hundred and even eighteen hundred percent—the sky is the limit. All that the traffic will bear. Uncle Sam has the money. Let's get it."[11]

General Butler then goes on to tell us about the profits made by the many corporations that produced for the war. Here we will mention just a few.

From 1910-1914, the average yearly earnings of the DuPont corporation was $6 million, but during the war years, 1914-1918, it made $58 million dollars a year, or a profit of 950 percent. Bethlehem Steel's average of $6 million a year between 1910 and 1914 jumped to an average of $49 million during 1914-1918. U.S. Steel's average yearly profits was $105 million in 1910-1914, but rose to $240 million annually from 1914-1918. Anaconda's average yearly profits leapt from $10 million in 1910-1914 to $34 million in 1914-1918. Utah Copper did even better: from $5 million to $21 million.[12]

President Wilson, who presided during the First World War, confided to Joseph Daniels, his Secretary of the Navy, that he was concerned that, "if America entered World War I, the great interests which control steel, oil, shipping, munitions factories and mines will of necessity become dominant factors, and when the war is over, our government will be in their hands. And Daniels later warned Roosevelt that if America did in fact enter the war, the power of Big Business would overwhelm the country.[13]

When President Dwight D. Eisenhower lay down the responsibilities of his office, he warned us to beware of the increasing power of the military-industrial complex. In a farewell speech, he said, "This conjunction of an immense military establishment and a large arms industry is new in the American experience...In the councils of government, we must guard against the acquisition of unwarranted influence, whether sought or unsought, by the military-industrial complex. The potential for the disastrous rise of misplaced power exists and will persist. We must never let the weight of this combination endanger our liberties or democratic processes. We should take nothing for granted."[14]

President Eisenhower went on to say, "Every gun that is made, every warship launched, every rocket fired, signifies in the final sense a theft from those who hunger and are not fed, those who are cold and are not clothed. This world in arms is not spending money alone, it is spending the sweat of its laborers, the genius of its scientists, the hopes of its children."[15]

As of September 2001, the U.S. had at least 725 military bases outside the country. "Slowly but surely," writes Chalmer Johnson, "the Department of Defense is obscuring and displacing the Department of State as the primary agency for making and administering foreign policy. We now station far more uniformed military officers in foreign countries than civilian diplomats, aid workers or environmental specialists."[16]

Taxes

The money to pay for the many needs of the civilian sector will have to come from the taxes the corporation avoid paying and the tax cuts doled out to them by various administrations. Many if not all of the corporations have been extremely skillful at not only avoiding taxes but also at dipping their hands into the Federal treasury to pull out hundreds of billions of dollars. For that purpose they have used numerous loopholes. They have used their influence in Congress to have their taxes drastically reduced. They have successfully lobbied Congress to pass all kinds of laws to provide them with all kinds of concessions and subsidies and they have used offshore islands to shelter from taxes their profits and other income. As a consequence, the hundreds of billions that are lost to the Federal treasury have been made up by increasing the many taxes, direct and indirect, paid by working people and especially by middle income working people [the so-called middle class].

" I'm for reporting them to the government.
They didn't declare half of their profits..."

The history of how business, especially Big Business, has avoided paying its fair share of taxes and depleted the federal treasury in numerous other ways would make even the Devil envious. Whereas before 1944, business paid nearly 50% of all taxes, by 2003, they paid only 7.4%.[17] During the 1950s business paid about 28% of all Federal taxes collected. Had it continued to pay the same share throughout the 60s and 70s, the Federal treasury would have gained $424.5 billion more than it did and there would have been a further savings on interests of an estimated $215 billion. Thus the savings in Federal tax policy from 1960-1980 deflected $639.5 billion from the U.S.

Treasury."[18] Between 1960 and 1979, the Federal debt grew by $616.9 billion. That just about equals the $639.5 billion in tax cuts that benefited Big Business and the big banks.[19] In 1992, the richest 1 million families paid $83.7 billion less in taxes than they would have paid were they taxed at the 1977 rate. That was because George Bush the father handed them a very generous tax cut.

From 1996 to 2000, years when the economy boomed and corporate profits soared, more than 60% of US Corporations paid no federal taxes – you read that correctly – no taxes.[20] About 70% of foreign owned companies doing business in the U.S reported that they did not owe any federal taxes during the late 1990's.[21] "Outside experts estimate that tax shelters cost the Federal Treasury at least $10 billion a year." It reported further that "aggressive use of tax shelters cost states as much as $12.4 billion in the year 2001.[22]

"The 257,000 taxpayers with incomes of more than $1 million received a bigger combined tax cut than the 85 million taxpayers received who make up the bottom 60% of the population. The modest tax cuts received by the great majority are in a fundamental sense, fraudulent. For those so-called supposed gains will be lost by severe program cuts which will fall mainly on Social Security, Medicare and Medicaid."[23]

It is the outrageously unfair tax system – a system that enriches the very wealthy while adding heavy tax burdens on both low and medium income working people – that must be addressed. It must be addressed so that the very wealthy individuals and tax-evading corporations must be made to pay a fair share. There will also have to be a stop to all the tax cuts and subsidies amounting to the hundreds of billions that are doled out mainly to Big Business. Once such measures are taken, the federal, state and local governments will have more of the needed money to carry out the sorely needed programs outlined above.

Pension Funds and Taxes That Will Be Paid in a Full Employment Economy

One very feasible way to attack unemployment is for working people to demand that the many billions of dollars of money accumulating in working people's pension funds be used for the building of public works, such as affordable housing, high-speed trains, solar energy, all levels of schools and above all, universal health care. Such invested dollars would provide appropriate interest rates for the funds' owners.

Another source of funds needed to carry out the vast public works for civilian purposes would come from the billions of dollars in taxes that will be paid by the millions of presently jobless workers who would be employed in a full-employment system.

Is Full Employment Possible?

Is the present system of our society ever capable of creating full employment? The answer is "Not likely" for as long as the very tools, land, equipment, factories, buildings and raw materials – the very means by which we sustain our lives – are owned largely by a small minority. As long as that minority owns the means of production and distribution, we will not have full employment. As we have shown in Chapter 6, mass unemployment is one of the crucial factors that make it possible for the capitalist class to reap most of the wealth and the power they possess.

You, the reader, having reached this point in the book, will ask, "Will any of the proposed solutions ever be carried out?" The answer is that they can be carried out only if there is a major shift in the balance of power. At present, it is the capitalist class that holds overwhelming power. It does so through the President, Congress and the Supreme Court. As pointed out earlier, and bears repeating, that class owns the factories and almost all of the other means that produce and distribute the goods and services. The wealth they derive from that ownership gives them overwhelming control over all three branches of government. Business interests have the huge amounts of money to pay for the very expensive election campaigns for the Presidency and the Congress. They also have the money to hire battalions of lobbyists to grease the palms of many of the key members of the House of Representatives and the Senate for the purpose of enacting many of the laws that promote their interests but which cause much adversity to the lives of most working people.

Business also uses its ownership of the television and print media to keep the minds of working people distracted by all kinds of programs, very few of which have anything to do with what really matters to working people.

As we have shown in Chapter 6, the capitalist class and especially its more wealthy members have a powerful interest in keeping large numbers of working people unemployed. What, one may therefore ask, will be the response if sufficient numbers of working people and their representatives start addressing the issue of mass unemployment with all the vigor it requires?

We do have what is supposed to be democratic elections, but the results of these elections invariably bring back to power either the Democrats or the Republicans. One can say for certain that the Republicans, who normally tend to represent Big Business, are certainly not interested in full employment. The majority of Democrats are simply indifferent to it or would at most give lip service to it, and then only when under pressure from working peoples' organizations.

Do either of the two major parties represent the real needs of working people?

First, most of the real leaders of both parties are headed by the top members of the capitalist class. Such leaders are hardly ever publicly exposed and they hide behind their nominees. And it is this leadership who decides who will be their parties' nominees for the Presidency and for Congress.

One could hardly expect such leaders to take any action against the interests of their class. No more proof is needed than the fact that both the Republicans and the Democrats excluded Ralph Nader, Patrick Buchanan and every other party from the campaign debates held before the last two elections.[24] The Republicans and the Democrats have for many decades been united in their determination to exclude from power anyone who might represent the interests of working people.

Secondly, election campaigns are heavily dependent on money, and are therefore fraught with corruption. The consequence is that mostly the wealthy of the capitalist class can afford to pour the required millions into the campaign chests of those candidates who they know will serve their interests.

Third, another very serious problem is that election day is one when working people have to be at work. After commuting to and from work, and working at jobs that leave most working people spiritually drained, few have the energy left to go out to vote. Why is it so difficult for Congress to enact a law that would make election day a holiday for all Americans? Is their inaction on this issue not proof that neither of the two major parties really care about democracy?

Fourth, there is very little in the campaigns of both major parties that addresses the real needs and concerns of working people.

Only Participation of All Working People in Progressive Politics Will Eliminate Mass Unemployment

The solution to the problem of mass unemployment in the U.S. depends on who wields the country's political power and for whose benefit. Will it continue to be the business class, whose representatives possess that power to make sure that mass unemployment will remain an enduring fact, or will it be authentic representatives of working people determined to create full employment with living wages?

How even one attempt to limit the business class domination of the economy ended in failure

Until the 1930s, the business class had always possessed the political power to run the economy as it saw fit. And it has always used its great power to maintain its control of the economy. But when in the 1930s, one out of four workers were hit by prolonged joblessness and many millions of others suffered pitifully lower paychecks, the business class was confronted by a serious attempt to reduce its power.

Because unemployment during the 1930s was so widespread, it was clear to many in the Roosevelt administration that only unconventional remedies could solve the acute and seemingly endless crisis. Among those remedies proposed by the Roosevelt administration was the establishment, in July 1935, of an agency within the Federal government that would plan the economy. That agency, the National Resources Planning Board (NRPB), was an attempt to limit the power of businessmen to control the economy for their exclusive benefit.

Its program consisted of four elements:

1- Industrial research and invention to be financed and controlled by the Federal government. Research conducted under government auspices would benefit all Americans, and not only the corporations. Patents on inventions discovered with the people's money would not be owned and hoarded by business, but would belong to the public.[25]

2- The motive behind the first element in the program was to eliminate the possibility that corporations would acquire and keep from development inventions that would enormously improve the lives of working people. An example in our time would be the resistance by energy corporations to the private and commercial use of solar and other forms of renewable energy, which would cost less and benefit the environment.

3- The third element of the NRPB program called for the more discriminating application and enforcement of the anti-trust laws. The government granted 70% of the huge World War II contracts to just 100 corporations and suspended anti-trust laws for the war's duration. The NRPB feared that so much power concentrated in corporate hands would corrupt the entire electoral process, the press, the educational system and finally the whole of society.

4- The fourth and perhaps most crucial element in the NRPB's program was the suggestion that the Federal government enter into certain crucial areas of the economy through the device of the 'mixed corporation.' Such corporations and industries would be those in which the government had already made enormous investments, in certain other industries in which expansion was deemed necessary, as well as in industries that were previously under alien control and most importantly in industries in which patents were crucial.

Direct government intervention in basic decision-making in crucial industries such as aluminum, magnesium, chemicals, shipbuilding, aviation, electric power, communications, etc., would go a long way toward solving the problem of monopoly control and would also create a democratic economy.[26]

These proposals posed a grave threat to the unfettered power of the business class to control the economy.

In 1943, when both houses of Congress came under Republican control, the House refused to provide the $1.4 million asked for by the NRPB. The Senate voted 44 to 31 to reduce NRPB's funding to $200,000. Later, the joint House and Senate conference required the NRPB to terminate its work by April 30, 1943 and to liquidate itself by the end of the year.

Leading the fight against the NRPB was Republican Senator Taft. He justified his opposition by saying,

"In my opinion they [the NRPB reports] are based on two policies and theories. The first is the theory of unlimited public spending and constant increase of the public debt after the war [World War II]. A policy of **deficit spending** is implicit in the measure the board (NRPB) proposes and in its attitude toward the spending of government money. In the second place, the board's plans are based on unlimited government interference in and regulation of all business activity, plus a very large amount of **government regulation** of what is now private industry."[27]

Senator Taft apparently forgot that at this very time, the government was "indulging" in massive **deficit spending** by pumping unprecedented billions of dollars into the coffers of the corporations that were producing the arms for the war, and that these corporations were amassing enormous profits from government contracts. Furthermore, the good Senator very conveniently failed to remember that it was the **lack of any**

government regulation of the business-controlled economy that brought about the crash and depression of the 1930s.

What lay behind the congressional Republicans' opposition to the NRPB?

"In 1943," wrote Philip H. White, "the wall [of the NRPB] fell in. It did not fall in rapidly with resounding reverberations, but it crumbled slowly under <u>somewhat mysterious pressures</u> (our emphasis)."[28] These mysterious pressures were exerted by none other than the major business groups determined to control the economy without any government interference.

Chief among those groups was the Business Advisory Council (BAC) created in 1933. Among its members were Henry I. Harriman, a prominent head of the U.S. Chamber of Commerce, Gerard Swope of General Electric, Alexander Legge of International Harvester and Walter Teagle of Standard Oil. Invitations to join were sent out to 41 eminent businessmen. The final membership consisted of several liberal executives from medium size firms. It also included a disproportionate number of businessmen from truly giant corporations, including Myron Taylor of U.S. Steel, Alfred Sloan of General Motors, Robert Wood of Sears Roebuck, Walter Gifford of AT&T. and Pierre DuPont of the DuPont Corporation. Gerard Swope of General Electric served as chairman.[29]

From the experience of the Great Depression, BAC leaders learned that the business class could not run the economy without federal support. The BAC now realized that only with the sustained and massive help of the federal government could their system be saved and prosper. Business leaders would accept badly needed and essential help from the government, but they wanted **no** government control. If the Federal government were allowed to plan and control the economy, it would, according to businessmen, curry favor with the voters by implementing a wide range of pro-worker reforms, among which full employment might well be its central focus.

The fact is that the business class does plan and run the U.S. economy, and it does so with the almost total cooperation of the Federal government. And it in fact plans the economy behind the mask of the Federal government. But its planning is such that it is often disastrous for the majority of working people, as well as for the long term health of the national economy.

Two Kinds of Proposals for Solving the Problem of Mass Unemployment

Two kinds of solutions have been proposed to create full employment.

The first kind accepts the capitalist system, but have called for many reforms that would create the conditions for full employment. Such proposals have been made mostly by some members of Congress. Two such proposals of the first kind, the 1945 Full Employment Bill and the 1976 Humphrey-Hawkins Bill have been discussed in Chapters 3 and 5, respectively. Since then, at least five other full employment bills have been introduced, all of which were buried in one or another House committee or subcommittee, chaired by a conservative congressman, usually a Republican or Southern Democrat.[30]

The latest of these Congressional proposals, H.R.1050 introduced in 1999 and sponsored by Congresswoman Barbara Lee of Oakland, was called A Living Wage, Jobs for All Act. Though H.R.1050 accepts the capitalist organization of the economy, it pinpoints the numerous problems afflicting the economy and also calls for their solutions through full employment.

Her proposal includes enacting into law the Economic Bill of Rights called for by President Franklin Roosevelt in 1944. That Bill of Rights included:

1- The right to a useful and remunerative job in the industries or shops or farms or mines of the nation.
2- The right to earn enough to provide an adequate living.
3- The right of every farmer to raise and sell farm products at a return which will provide a decent family living.
4- The right of every business, large or small, to trade in an atmosphere of freedom from unfair competition and domination by monopolies at home or abroad.
5- The right of every family to a decent home.
6- The right to adequate medical care and the opportunity to achieve and enjoy good health.
7- The right to adequate protection from the economic fears of old age, sickness, accident and unemployment.
8- The right to a good education.

She also called for updating an extending the 1944 "Economic Bill of Rights" by including the following:

1- Every adult American able and willing to earn a living through paid work has the right to a free choice among opportunities for useful and productive paid employment (part time or full time) at decent real wages or for self-employment.
2- Every adult American unable to work for pay or to find employment has the right to an adequate standard of living that rises with increases in the wealth and productivity of the society.

The proposed law, like some of those that preceded it, called not only for decent jobs for all at a living wage, but also the support systems that would allow all persons to take on a job as well as to perform the job as efficiently as required. This means that all working people, even before they start their working lives, need a living income, decent housing and adequate health services. In addition, H.R. 1050 called for the implementation of the watered down Full Employment Act of 1946 and of the Humphrey-Hawkins Act of 1976, both of which have been mostly ignored by subsequent administrations.[31]

Her proposal, therefore, called for income security for those unable to work, a decent income for family farmers, and a good education for all, which would include not only reading, writing and arithmetic but also reasoning and responsibility, both of the latter badly needed in most of our public schools.

Proposals Offered by Economic Democrats

The second kind, offered by Economic Democrats, call for full participation of working people in the decisions affecting the nation's economy. They see this as an indispensable condition for the creation of full employment

One of the most comprehensive proposals for the democratic planning of the economy was offered by Michael Harrington, a democratic socialist in an article published in 1984. Basing his proposals on legislation written by Bertram Gross, a specialist on full employment, he called for both a listing of national needs to be drawn up with the broadest participation of ordinary people. Such legislation would also provide information for technical proposals to be developed by experts, as well as analysis of the total input and output of the national economy based entirely upon social needs as opposed to narrow private needs. The listing of national needs would be used as a basis for industrial policy and planning for full employment. [32]

Economic democrats first point to the sheer irrationality of a system which goes well beyond "the contrast between opulence for a few and poverty and hardship for the many."[33] Working people need to envision an entirely new way of organizing the nation's economy. All working people and that includes scientists, engineers, technicians, teachers, firemen, doctors, nurses, etc. – in short all whose main income derives from working for wages or salaries – need to recognize that they are the ones that are already doing all the necessary work of the economy but doing it in accord with the narrow goals and interests of the capitalist class.

Those goals are laid down mostly by the chief executive officers of the nation's corporations. They decide what, how and for what purpose goods and services are to be produced. Overwhelmingly, the purpose is to create as much profit as possible to distribute as dividends to investors. It is important to note, as mentioned in Chapter 7, that more than 80% of all corporate shares are owned by a very small percentage of investors.

It is no accident that the workers have no voice in what, how, and why anything is produced and how services are rendered. Through their CEOs, the major owners of corporations have fought tenaciously to keep out workers and their unions from any decisions affecting production and services. When workers are so excluded, corporate leaders are free to hire and fire their employees, free to export jobs, free to introduce technology to displace their employees, free to merge with other corporations so as to lay off no longer needed workers, and free to produce poor quality, short-lived and health-risky goods, and to reduce wages, salaries and benefits at will.

What keeps workers mostly passive and indifferent to what, how and why those goods are produced is the need for most of them to keep their jobs and avoid falling into the pit of unemployment, so that they are able to meet their needs and those of their families.

It is mainly this fear of falling into the degradation of joblessness that fuels their performance at the workplace. For if, as is the case, most workers gain very little sense of self-fulfillment and satisfaction from their work, how else, but the fear of unemployment can make them tolerate work that stifles their dormant creative impulses.

It is therefore no accident that workers are so relieved when the work week ends that they greet each other TGIF, "Thank God It's Friday." And neither is it an accident that some wit came up with "If you don't believe that people return from the dead, just look at working people at quitting time."

Now all those circumstances are all part and parcel of the system under which working people labor. To reinforce the economic part of the system, workers very early in their lives are put into situations where they are made to compete with one another. At all levels of our school system, whether in sports activities or in the way the students are graded, working class students are made to feel that they are in competition with one another. This is continued at the workplace where competition among various levels of employees is fostered by organizing them in the form of a hierarchy – workers, foremen, technicians, supervisors, and managers.

But whereas workers are thus led to believe and to feel that they are competing with one another, business people have always bitterly hated competing with one another and have tried hard to eliminate it.[34]

It has in fact always been cooperation and not competition that has advanced the interests and happiness of people everywhere. Take any project such as the construction of a large mall. To achieve the right result, it takes the tight cooperation of the architect, the contractor, the carpenters, electricians, plumbers, painters, tile layers, as well as the semi-skilled and unskilled laborers. What, for instance, would any music sound like if the members of a symphonic orchestra do not cooperate, no matter how skillful the maestro? But the most telling proof of the benefit of cooperation is when corporate chief executive officers require their subordinates to be team players – another way of saying that they expect them to cooperate fully in achieving the objectives of the corporations. Furthermore, corporations have organized "quality of life circles" among their rank and file workers in an effort to tap into their creative impulses for any ideas that would improve their companies' efficiency and thereby their profitability. Is this not a roundabout way of gaining the cooperation of their employees?

But beyond even such examples, all the great advances of humanity occurred not through competition, which have led to recurrent wars of great devastation and vast loss of lives, but to cooperation. A classic example from recent history is the competition between Germany and her rivals that led to the Second World War. Subsequently, the cooperation between them made it possible for both Germany and Japan to rebuild their economies of both former enemies.

We are also exposed to a barrage of ideas intended to reinforce our thinking that competition is beneficial. One of those ideas is that humans are inherently greedy. If people are inherently greedy, why is it that those who work at something they love doing are in fact often surprised that they are paid for it? The cause for this surprise is the sense of personal fulfillment and happiness they derive from their work. Many people such as independent artists, craftsmen, technicians, scientists and even such workers as independent carpenters, plumbers, etc. may derive enough pleasure from their work thus making it unlikely for them to be greedy.

Most working people, if they do feel compelled to accumulate assets of one kind or another, do so to hedge against the very insecurity that is caused by a system that treats a job as a privilege or an opportunity rather than a right. At the top of the income pyramid, money and other assets simply accumulate with hardly any effort. Big money, being big, can more easily bear losses when the stock market is at a downturn and often win again with better results during upturns.

Once workers are freed from the fear of unemployment, their energies will inspire them to produce products and services far more useful to society than are presently produced. Free of the concern to produce quarterly profits for the capitalist class, they would produce goods such as cars that would last much longer and use far less energy. They would also avoid producing the kinds of food that result in heart and other diseases. Inspired by a sense that they are serving the common wealth and welfare, the presently dormant creative impulses of working people will flower resulting in far more improvements and inventions than those created under the present system. In general, they would also make production decisions far more beneficial for all.

Contrary to what some people may think, most workers in all categories are far more intelligent than is required for full participation in a system of economic democracy.[35]

Endnotes

Introduction: How the Public is Deceived

1   Statistical Abstract of the U.S. 2004-2005, p.329
2   Cited in Ibid p.328
3   Cited in Ibid p.311
4   Statistical Anstract of the U.S. 2003, p.327
5   Cited in Ibid p.324
6   The CTJ Newsletter, September 2004
7   Statistical Abstract of the U.S. 2004-2005, p.328
8   Lewis Lapham. Notebook: Winter of Discontent. 1992
9   Richard Yates. Why Unions Matter, copyright by Monthly Review Press. 1998
10 Andrew Strom, U.S. Labor Law: How the United States' Stacked Labor Laws make it nearly impossible to gain union representation. Dollars & Sense, Sept-Oct 2003, p.45
11 Richard L. Trumka, Defeating Scab Culture, in Democratic Left, Sept.-Oct., 1991, p.32
12 Michael H. Leroy and John H. Johnson IV, Death by Legal Injunction: National Emergency Strikes Under the Taft-Hartley Act and the Moribound Right to Strike. Arizona Law Review, Spring 2001 p.2
13 Ibid p.26 and Note #23
14 Bill Moyers, Inequality Matters, cited in Labor Party Press, July-Aug. 2004, Vol. 9.

Chapter 1: The Extent of Unemployment and Underemployment

1   Lester Thurow, Crusade That's Killing Prosperity, The American Prospect, March-April 1996, pp. 54-59.

2   Mark Zeperzauer and Arthur Naiman, Take the Rich off Welfare, 1996. See also Chapter 7 for more details on corporate welfare.

3   Lester Thurow: The Crusade that's Killing Prosperity, American Prospect, March-April 1996 p.56.

4   Michael Yates, Longer Hours, Fewer Jobs, Employment in the U. S. Monthly Review Press

5   Dollars and Sense May-June 1995

6   Bureau of the Census, 2003 American Community Survey.

7   Statistical Abstract of the U.S. !999

8   People's Weekly World, April 10, 1993

9   New York Times, Jan, 31, 2000

10   Newsweek, Sept. 23, 1994

11   Newsweek, Sept. 13, 1991, p.41

12   Labor Notes, April 1992, p.

13   Michael Yates, Us Versus Them, Laboring in the Academic Factory, Monthly Review, Jan. 2000, p42 Yates provides a detailed expose of the causes and consequences of the debasement of the status of faculty in America's institutions of higher learning.

Chapter 2: The Sharp Conflict of Interest Between Working People and their Employers That Preceded the Assault and Defeat By the Representatives of The Business Class of the Full Employment Law Proposal of 1945

1   Arthur Schlesinger, The Coming of the New Deal, p.404-405

2   Priscilla Murolo and A.B.Chitty, A Short Illustrated History of Labor in the U.S. p.148

3   Joseph G. Rayback: A history of American Labor, p.304

4   William Foster: American Trade Unionism, 1947, p.107

5   Priscilla Murolo and A.B. Chitty: A Short Illustrated History of Labor in the U. S. p.148.

6   Schlesinger, p.138
7   Ibid p.138
8   American Social History Project (ASHP): Who Built America?
     Working People and the Nation's Economy, Politics, Culture
     and Society, Vol. 2, p.355
9   Ibid p.355
10   Nelson Lichtenstein: State of the Union, A Century of Amer-
     ican Labor. 2002, p.37
11   Ibid p.37
12   Richard Boyer and Herbert Morais: Labor's Untold Story,
     p.237
13   Ibid p.238
14   Ibid p.238
15   Ibid p.49
16   Ibid p.51
17   Ibid p.59
18   Rayback p.360
19   Lichtenstein p.39
20   American Social History Project: Who Built America, Vol. 2,
     1992, p.415
21   Ibid p.418
22   Ibid p.418
23   Ibid p.418
24   Rayback pp.277-278
25   American Social History Project, p.431
26   Jeremy Brecher: Strike, p.240
27   Ibid p.243
28   Ibid p.244
29   Ibid p.245

Chapter 3: The Assault and Defeat of the 1945 Full Employment Law Proposal by the Representatives of the Business Class

1   Many of the background facts and comments dealing with the full Employment Law Proposal of 1945 have drawn heavily from Stephen Kemp Bailey, Congress Makes A Law. It is no exaggeration to say the Bailey wrote the definitive work on this law. In this author's opinion, Bailey's book is a majestic and magnificent piece of work. The full text of the bill as originally introduced may be found in Bailey's book: Appendix A, pp 243-248.

2   All the above quotes are from U.S. Congress, House Hearings on S380, 79th Congress, Vol. 1171, p. 548

3   Ibid, p.551

4   Andrew Hacker, Ed., The Corporate Take-Over, 1964 p.185

5   David Vogel: Why Businessmen Distrust Their State, British Journal of Political Science, 1978, p.54.

6   Harry Magdoff, Are There Lessons to Be Learned, in Monthly Review, February 1991, pp.16-17.

7   Bailey, pp. 135-137

8   Ibid, pp137-138

9   Ibid pp. 138-142

10 U.S. Congress House Hearings on S380, Congress Vol. 1071, p. 458.

11 Ibid, p. 468

12 Ibid, p. 472

13 Rexford Tugwell; In Search of Roosevelt, 1972

14 U.S. Congress House Hearins on S380, 79th Congress, Vol. P. 473.

15 Ibid, 474.

16 Ibid, 474.

17 Ibid, pp. 481-483.

18 Molly Ivins, Chamber of Criminals, The Progressive, Sept. 1999, p, 46

19 Stephen Kemp Bailey, Congress Makes a Law. pp. 143-145.
20 Ibid, p.146.
21 Ibid, 1. 147
22 U.S. Congress, House Hearinfs on S380, 79th Congress Vol. 1071, p. 739.
23 Ibid, p. 741.
24 Ibid, p. 755.
25 Ibid, 741
26 Ibid, p. 742
27 Ibid, p. 743
28 Kim Mc Quaid, Big Business and President Power: From FDR to Reagan, 1982, pp.125-126.
29 Ibid, pp. 127-128.
30 Ibid, pp.129

Chapter 4: How the Capitalist Class Was Able To Scuttle the Full Employment Law Proposal of 1945

1   These facts have been documented in many publications dealing with the early New Deal years. On these matters, readers may wish to consult two especially good books. Barton J. Bernstein, The New Deal: The Conservative Achievements of Liberal Reform in Barton J. Bernstein (ed) Towards a New Past (1963). and Paul K. Conkin, The New Deal, 1967
2   Harold L. Ickes, Secret Diary of Harold L. Ickes, Vol.1, 1933-1936, p.31
3   Rexford Tugwell, In Search of Roosevelt, 1972 p. 267
4   Gabriel Kolko, Main Currents in Modern American History, p. 312
5   Historical Statistics of the Unites States, 1975, Vol. 2. p. 925

[6]   Gabriel Kolko, Main Currents in Modern American History, p. 312

[7]   Ibid, pp. 312-313

[8]   Ibid, p. 313

[9]   V.O.Key, Politics, Parties and Pressure Groups, Fifth Edition, 1964

[10] Stephen Kemp Bailey: Congress Makes A Law, p. 185

[11] Ibid p. 186

[12] Ibid p. 187

[13] Rexford Tugwell: In Search of Roosevelt

Chapter 5: The Opposition of the Business Class to the 1978 Humphrey-Hawkins Full Employment Bill And the Response of the Bill's Most Prominent Supporters and The Early Burial by Congress of Five Full Employment Law Proposals Between 1985 and 1998

[1]   Gary Mucciaroni, The Political Failure of Employment Policy 1945-1982.

[2]   See the chapter on Recessions for a more detailed analysis of the causes of the Great Depression.

[3]   Gary Mucciarone, p. 95.

[4]   Ibid p.100

[5]   Cited in Ibid p.97.

[6]   See Chapter 3 for the composition of the NAM and the COC.

[7]   Bertram M. Grossman: Job Rights Under American Capitalism.Social Policy, Jan-Feb.1975. (Mr. Grossman was distinguished professor of urban affairs)

[8]   Leon Keyserling: The Problem of High Unemployment. Policy Studies Journal, Vol.8, Winter 1979,No.3,p.349

[9]   Statement of Lewis W. Foy, 95th Congress, Vol. 10, p.229-231.

[10] Rexford Tugwell, In Searh of Roosevelt , p145, 1972

[11] See my introduction chapter for a discussion of the Taft-Hartley Act.

[12] See Hagedorn statement, 95th Congress vol. 10 p. 242.

[13] Ibid, p.245.

[14] Ibid, p.247

[15] Ibid, p.64

[16] Ibid p. 64

[17] Ibid p. 65

[18] Ibid p. 190

[19] Ibid p.191

[20] Ibid p.191

[21] Ibid p.192-193

[22] Ibid p.192-193

[23] Ibid p.193

[24] Ibid p.968

[25] Ibid p.169

[26] Ibid p.170

[27] Ibid p.172

[28] Ibid p.172

[29] Congress person Lynn Woolsey to the author

Chapter 6: Why are capitalists as a class opposed to full employment?

[1] See chapter on the export of jobs on the exploitation by mainly big businesses of a vast unemployed work force in developing countries all for the purpose of avoiding paying good wages and good working conditions to American workers. And incredibly, they do this with the aid of the federal government.

[2] Robert Lekachman, The Specter of Full Employment, Harpers, February 1977, p.36

[3] Business Week, December 21, 1981

4 Michael Kalecki, Political Aspects of Full Employment, The Political Quarterly, ()ct-Dec. 1943 Vol. X1V, No.4.

5 Robert Lekachman, The Specter of Full Employment, Harpers, February 1977, p. 36

6 Lester Thurow, The Crusade That's Killing Prosperity, The American Prospect, March-April 1996

7 Pierre Bowrdieu, Frederic Lebaron and Gerard Mauger, Le Monde Jan. 17, 1998, Cited by Katha Pollitt, The Nation, March 2, 1998, p.9

Chapter 7: The Great and Increasing Disparity in Income & Wealth as A Cause of Mass Unemployment

1 Arthur MacEwan, Should We Be Concerned About the Great Disparity in Wealth, Dollars and Sense, Sept.-Oct. 1998, p.37

2 California C10 News, January 30, 1987

3 Sam Rosenberg: Restructuring the Labor Force, The Role of Government Policies, in Robert Cherry et al: The Imperiled Economy, Book 2, 1988.

4 Chris Tilly, Regenerating Inequality, Robert Cherry et al: The Imperiled Economy, Book 2,1988).

5 Kevin Phillips: The Politics of Rich and Poor, Cited in Political Affairs, October 1990.

6 Interview with Tony Mazzochi, Z Magazine, January 1995.

7 Cited in Political Affairs, June 1991

8 Business Week, Sept 1, 1997

9 Jesse Jackson: The Coming Collision The Progressive Populist, August 1998.

10 Cited in Economic Notes, Oct. 1997

11 Robert Reich, It's the Year 2000 Economy Stupid. The American Prospect, Jan.3, 2003 p. 64.

12 Holly Sklar, $1.3 trillon, Coffers of Forbes 400 San Francisco Examiner, Oct. 16, 2000.

13 Cited in People's Weekly World, July 14, 2001

14 Molly Ivins: The progressive.

15 Jim West, Cream for the Rich, Dregs for the Poor, Review of Kevin Phillips' book, The Politics of Rich

16 Molly Ivins, If Robber Baron Shoes Fit, The Progressive Populist. Aug. 2001.

17 Cited in Political Affairs June 1991.

18 Chuck Collins et al, Shifting Fortunes, The Perils of the Growing Wealth Gap 1999.

19 Cited in Political Affairs, June 1991

20 Cited In Ibid, June 1991

21 Bob Herbert, Living on Borrowed Money, N.Y. Times, Nov. 10, 2003

22 Holly Sklar, The Value of Minimum Wage Declines, The North Bay Progressive, June 27-July 24, 2003.

23 Nathan Newman, Restore the Minimum Wage, The Progressive Populist Oct. 2003.

24 Associated Press, CEO's Get Raises as Workers Get the Axe, N.Y. Times Aug. 28, 2001 p.4.

25 Chuck Collins et al: The Perils of the Growing Wealth Gap 1999.

26 Time Magazine, Nov. 9, 1998

27 New York Times, Nov. 10, 2003

28 Donald C. Bartlett and James B. Steele, Corporate Welfare, Time Magazine, Nov. 9, 1998.

29 Ibid , Time Magazine, Nov. 16, 199.

30 Michael Beard, A History of Capitalism 1500-1980, 1983.

31 See Chapter 6 for a more detailed account of the technological advances of the 1990's.

32 Gabriel Kolko, Main Currents in Modern American History, p.102-103. Almost all the data relating to the 1920's may be found in Kolko's book.

33 Ibid p. 103

34 Ibid p.103.

[35] See Chapter 12 on recessions for more details.
[36] See Chapter 9 on the effects of advance technology on un-employment.
[37] Cited in Chuck Collins et al, Shifting Fortunes, The Perils of the Growing Wealth Gap 1999.

Chapter 8: Business's Unending Introduction and Use of Advanced Technology As a Cause of Mass Unemployment

[1] The Washington Spectator, Vol. 11, No 1, January 1 1985
[2] Laurence Zeitlin, Professor of Industrial Psychology in a letter to the New York Times, July 29, 1984
[3] People's World, June 14, 1980
[4] Jeremy Rifkin. The End of Work, 1995, p.134
[5] Ibid. p.75
[6] Ibid. p.135
[7] Ibid. p.75
[8] Ibid. p.76
[9] Ibid. p.136
[10] Ibid. p.137
[11] Ibid. p.137
[12] Ibid. p.137
[13] Ibid. p.138
[14] Ibid. p.141
[15] Ibid. p.144
[16] David Breen, Letter to the New York Times, July 28, 1992
[17] Jeremy Rifkin. The End of Work, 1995, p.145
[18] Ibid. p.149
[19] Ibid. p.149
[20] Ibid. p.152
[21] Ibid. p.153
[22] Ibid. p.155
[23] Ibid. p.157

24 Simon Head, The New Ruthless Economy, *The New York review of Books*, Feb 29, 1996

25 Laurence Zeitlin, letter to the *N.Y. Times*, July 29, 1984

26 *The Washington Spectator*, Vol.11, No,1, January 1, 1985

27 *Political Affairs*, February 1986

28 Herb Mills, The Men Along the Shore, *San Francisco Chronicle*, September 7, 1980

29 Sylvia Nassar, Clinton Job Plan in Manufacturing Meets Skepticism, *New York Times*, Dec., 27, 1992

30 Ibid, December 27, 1992

31 Elizabeth Becker. You can go home again, but a farmer's sons find it is not so profitable. *New York Times*, December 1, 2003

32 Ben Lilliston and Niel Ritchie. Freedom to Fail: How U.S. Farming policies have helped agribusinesses and pushed family farmers towards extinction. *International Monitor*, July-August 2000.

33 Thimothy Egan. Amid Dying Plains Towns . . . *New York Times*, December 1, 2003.

34 Jeremy Rifkin. *The End of Work*, 1995, p?

35 Jeremy Rifkin. *The End of Work*, 1995, p.70-71

Chapter 9: The Export of Jobs as a Major Cause of Mass Unemployment

1 Multinational Monitor, March 9, 1997

2 Leia Raphaelidas: "Sewing Discontent in Nicaragua," *Multinational Monitor*, September, 1997

3 Jennifer Tung: "Coming Apart at the Seam," *New York Post*, Sept. 23, 1999

4 *National Labor Committee Press Release*, November 18, 1999

5 Ibid., November 18, 1999.

6 Ibid., November 18, 1999.

7   Ibid., March 2001
8   Ibid., November 18, 1999
9   *New York Times*, July 21, 1995
10   *People's Weekly World*, October 31, 1992
11   *People's World*, July 23, 1980
12   *Wall Street Journal*, July 23, 1980
13   Bluestone and Harrison: *Capital and Communities* , pp41, 20
14   *U.S. News and World Report*, October 10,1980
15   *Wall Street Journal*, September 23, 1980
16   *New York Times*, November 29,1976
17   *New York Times*, September 21, 1980
18   *New York Times*, September 14, 1980
19   *Political Affairs*, August 1991
20   *The Nation*, May 20 1991
21   *Wall Street Journal*, March 11, 1981
22   Peggy Musgrave, *Direct Investment Abroad and the Multi-nationals*
23   Bluestone, Harrison and Baker, *Corporate Flight*
24   Robert Scott, "NAFTA at Seven, The Economic Policy Institute, cited in *Labor Party Press*, July 2001
25   *New York Times*, June 24, 1998.
26   *New York Times*, June 24, 1998.
27   William Greider, *One World Ready or Not*, p. 116
28   Ibid, p. 91
29   *The Nation*, May 23, 1997
30   *The Nation*, February 17 1997
31   *United Electrical News*, May 23, 1997
32   Wayne M. O'Leary: "Real Solutions to Outsourcing," The Progressive Populist, May 15 2004, Copyright by Ampersand Publishing Co. 220 W. Railroad St. Storm Lake Iowa, 50588
33   *Political Affairs*, August 1991
34   *Sweatshop Watch Newsletter*, Spring 2001.

35 *Multinational Monitor*, January/February 1993
36 "Aiding and Abetting Corporate flight, U.S. AID in the Caribbean Basin," By Barbara Briggs, *Multinational Monitor*, January/February, 1993
37 *Multinational Monitor*, March, 1997, p. 22
38 Cited in *People's Daily World*, October 17, 1992, p.17
39 For an excellent view of how and why corporations operate, see William M. Dugger: *Corporate Hegemony*, 1989, Greenwood Press
40 Dollars & Sense, March 1991
41 Ibid., March 1991
42 *The Washington Spectator*, November 1984
43 Barbara Briggs: "Aiding and Abetting Corporate Flight" *Multinational Monitor*. Jan-Feb. 1993
44 *Viewpoint* No.4 (1975), "AFL-CIO Industrial Union Department," Cited in Melman, p.35
45 "National Labor Committee Education Fund in Support of Worker and Human Rights in Central America." Cited in *Peoples' Weekly World*, Oct. 31, 1992
46 *The Progressive Populist*, May 15, 2001
47 *Pacific Sun*, November 10-16, 1993
48 Ibid., November 10-16, 1993
49 Ibid., November 10-16, 1993
50 *Dollars & Sense*, March 1991

Chapter 10: Mergers and Acquisitions as A Cause of Mass Unemployment

1   E.K. Hunt: *An Economic History of the USA*
2   Paul Baran and Paul Sweezy: *Monopoly Capitalism*, p.36. While price cutting competition for businessman have mostly been eliminated, the competition among working people is to this day very much alive and well, thanks to the efforts of the business class. American workers have to compete

not only with their fellow citizens but also with workers all over the world who earn abysmally low wages.

3   Douglas Dowd: *The Twisted Dream*, p.126

4   Benton Gup Ed: *Megamergers in a Global Economy*

5   Douglas Dowd: *The Twisted Dream*, p.128

6   Ibid p.128

7   E.K. Hunt: *An Economic History of the USA*

8   Sylvia Porter: How the U.S. Promotes mergers in *S.F. Chronicle*, May 13, 1982

9   *U.E. News*. January 14, 1985.p.6

10   *Economic Notes:* December 1997

11   Robert Samuelson: The Mysterious Merger Frenzy, *Newsweek*. October 16, 2000, p.55

12   Micheal Beaud: *A History of Capitalism* 1500-1980

13   Reinhard Bendix: Work and Authority in Industry, p.27. Cited in E.K. Hunt: *History of Economics Through a Critical Perspective* 1979.

14   Ibid:p.37

15   Cited in E.K. Hunt. Ibid p.55

16   Ibid p.56

17   Edward Bernstein: *What's Ahead*,1984

18   Douglas Dowd: *The Twisted Dream*

19   *Northern California Labor News*. December 14, 1979

20   Ibid: December 14, 1979

21   Douglas Dowd: *Capitalism and its Economics* 2000 Pluto Press

22   Brad Marks: Megamergers Lengthen Unemployment Lines, *Electronic Media*. December 10, 2001

23   *Congressional Quarterly Researches*: Jobs in the 90's. February 29, 1992, p.10

24   *N.Y. Times, January 4, 1999*

25   A.V. Krebs: *The Progressive Populist*. January 1999. P.6

26   *N.Y. Times, January 13, 1999*

27 Martha Gruelle" Nurses Fight Hospital Reengineering, *Labor Notes*, October 1995.p.5

27a Susan C. Faludi, Safeway LBO Yields Vast Profits But Exacts a Heavy Human Toll , Wall Street Journal May 16 1990.

28 Hearings Before a Subcommittee of the Committee on Government Operations, House of Representatives, 100th Congress, First Session , March 3 and June 1987, Pp 4 and 18

29 Ibid, p.22

30 Walter B. Kissinger: The World of Takeovers, Pernicious, *N.Y. Times*. December 5, 1986

Chapter 11: Import of Labor as a Cause of Mass Unemployment

1 David Bacon, How U.S. Corporations Won the Immigrant Debate, *Z Magazine*, Nov. 2004, p.34

2 *Time*, Sept. 20, 2004, p.58

3 Ibid., p.59

4 Ibid., p.62

5 Steven A. Camarota, A Jobless Recovery? Immigrant Gains and Native Losses, *Center for Immigration Studies*, October 2004

6 Dr. George J. Borjas, Increasing the Supply of Labor Through Immigration, Measuring the Impact on Native-born Workers, *Center for Immigration Studies*, May 2004, p.1

7 *Business Week*, March 10, 2003, p.82

8 Ibid., p. 83

9 Ibid., p.82

10 Alexander Nguyen, High Tech Migrant Labor, *The American Prospect*, Dec. 20, 1998, p.41

11 Ibid., p.41

12 *Business Week*, March 10, 2003, p.82

Chapter 12: The Federal Reserve Bank as a Creator of Mass Unemployment

1   Mark Breibart and Gerald Epstein: "The Power of the Fed," *The Progressive*, April 1983. P 32
2   William Greider *Keepers of the Temple*, p.57. Much of the following facts are taken from this superb book.
3   Ibid p.682
4   Cited in Robert Lekachman: "Volkenized," *The Nation Magazine*, Nov. 3, 1979, p.420
5   Much if not all the facts related to the consequences of interest rates increase during the Reagan administration are taken from the superb work of William Greider, *Keepers of the Temple*...
6   Ibid, p.588
7   Ibid, p.590
8   Ibid , p. 590
9   Ibid p. 585
10 Ibid , p.586
11 See chapter 10 for more details
12 Robert Lekachman: Managing inflation in a full employment society, *Annals of the American Academy*, March 1975
13 Edward Bernstein, What's Ahead, *Industrial Publishers*, New York 1984
14 Robert Lekachman, Managing Inflation in a full employment society, *Annals of the American Academy*, March 1975, p. 418

Chapter 13: Recessions as a Cause for Mass Unemployment

1   see Chapter 7 for a detailed discussion of how this ever-growing income and wealth inequality creates mass unemployment.
2   See chapter 8 for a detailed discussion.

3   See chapter 9 for a detailed account of job exports and its impact on unemployment.
4   See chapter 10 for a detailed discussion.
5   See the chapter on the role of the Federal Reserve Bank in creating unemployment.
6   *San Francisco Chronicle* June 5, 2001
7   *New York Times,* May 5, 2001
8   Ibid, May 5, 2001
9   *New York Times,* May 5, 2001
10 Ibid, May 5, 2001
11 *Time,* April 16, 2001 p. 40
12 Ibid, p.38
13 Ibid, p.40
14 Richard O. Boyer and Herbert M. Morais. *Labor's Untold Story,* p.249
15 Nancy E Rose: *Put to work, Relief Programs in the Great Depression,* p.18
16 Joseph Rayback: *A History of American Labor,* 1966, p. 313-314
17 Cited in Stephen Kemp Bailey: *Congress Makes a Law,* pp.6,7
18 Quoted in Harold M. Mayer and Richard C. Wade. Chicago, "Growth of a Metropolis," p.358. Cited in T.H. Watkins, *The Hungry Years,* 1999.
19 We shall see in Chapter 12 how the "free enterprise" system is controlled and manipulated so as to avoid a similar catastrophic depression, all at the expense of working people.
20 For extensive accounts of the widespread human misery brought about by the Great Depression, see Studs Terkel's "Hard Times."
21 Cited in William K. Klingaman: 1929, *The Year of the Great Crash,* 1989.
22 A detailed account of the Reagan recession is provided in Chapter 12.

23 *Newsweek.*, January 13, 1992, p. 18

24 Ibid., January 13, 1992, p. 18

25 Newsweek quoting Paul Hirsh, a professor of strategy and organization at Northwestern University. *Newsweek* January 13, 1992, p.22

26 *Dollars & Sense* July-August, 2002, p. 11

27 *Dollars & Sense*, November 1992, p. 23

28 *Dollars & Sense*, November 1992, p. 13

Chapter 14: The Outrageous Consequences of Mass Unemployment

1 Richard D. Vogel. Capitalism and Incarceration Revisited, *Monthly Review*, September 2003, p.43

2 Julia Lutsky, Incarceration USA. *People's Weekly World*, Sept. 13, 1997

3 Fox Butterfield. Crime down, but prison costs up, *San Francisco Chronicle*, July 28, 2003

4 Christian Parenti. The "New" Criminal Justice System, *Monthly Review*, July-August 2001, p. 25

5 Richard D. Vogel, Capitalism and Incarceration Revisited. Monthly Review, Sept. 2003, p.40

6 Christian Parenti, The New Criminal Justice System. *Monthly Review*, July-August 291, p.23

7 *San Francisco Chronicle*, March 4, 1985

8 Richard D. Vogel. Capitalism and Incarceration Revisited, *Monthly Review*, September 2003. p.38)

9 Editorial in *the Nation magazine*, February 20, 1995

10 Curt Anderson. U.S. Crime Rate for 2002 hit lowest level in 30 years, *San Francisco Chronicle*, August 25, 2002

11 N.R. Kentfield with Michael Marriot. On Stolen Wheels: New York Youth Defy Authority. *N.Y. Times*, August 10, 1992

12 *N.Y. Times* Vol. CVII No.92, Sept. 1981

[13]   Evelyn Nieves. Funeral Held For Mother who was slain *N.Y. Times*, November 12, 1992

[14]   Susan Litwin. An American Tragedy, Why Mass Murders are on the Rise, *McCalls* July 1994

[15]   Andrew H. Malcolm. Deaths on the Iowa Prairie and New Victims of Economy. *N.Y. Times*. December. 10, 1986

[16]   *S.F. Chronicle*, November 3, 1999

[17]   *S.F. Chronicle*, August 29, 2003

[18]   Editorial in the Nation October 18, 1993

[19]   Ford Fessender, Study Produces Portrait of U. S. Rampage Killers, *S.F. Chronicle*, April 19, 2002

[20]   Editorial in the *Nation*, October 18, 1993

[21]   Ralph A. Catalono, Samuel L. Lind & Abram B. Rosenblatt. Unemployment and Foster Home placements. *American Journal of Public Health*, Vol.89 #6, June 1999

[22]   Associate Press. Child Abuse on Rise in State. *Marin Independent Journal*, January 7, 1996

[23]   U. S. News and World Report. February 3, 1997

[24]   *San Francisco Chronicle*, October 6, 1999

[25]   Press Release, Marin, California Chapter of the National Organization of Women, October 1993

[26]   Jaxon Van Derbeken. Slain Boy's Mom had sought help, San Francisco Chronicle July 1, 2003

[27]   Ryam Kim. Behind Family Massacres, San Francisco Chronicle, November 17, 2002

[28]   Shulamit Lala Ashensber Straussuer and Norman Kolko Phillips. The Impact of Jobless on Professionals and Managerial Employees and their Families, Families in Society, Vol. 80 #6, November-December 1999

[29]   *Business Week*, May 13, 1991

[30]   Bob Herbert. Change the Channel, *New York Times*, December 19, 2003

[31]   *Newsweek*, January 7, 1985

[32] Michael Janofsky and Nick Madigan, Wildfire Heats Racial Tension, *San Francisco Chronicle*, July 2, 2002

[33] Nicholas K. Geranios of AP, Firefighters – Arsonist on the Ranks, San Francisco Chronicle, July 4 2002

[34] Associated Press, Armored Car Suspect Feared Losing his job, *Marin Independent Journal*, November 30, 1997

[35] *SF Chronicle*, November 6, 1981

[36] *Economic Notes*, January 1998

[37] Francis X. Clines. Appeals for Peace in Ohio after 2 Days of Protest, *New York Times*, April 12, 2001

[38] Lorena Oropeza. Making History, *The Chicano Movement Occasional Paper*, No. 17, December 1997

[39] www.Nationmaster.com/encyclopedia/1992-Los Angeles-riots, June 16, 2005

[40] The 2003 Calendar Celebrating Americas "Thin Blue Line"

[41] David Gonzales. Seeking Security, Many Retreat Behind Bars and Razor Wires, *New York Times*, January 17, 1993, p.1

[42] *Economic Notes*, November 1997

[43] *Dollars and Sense*, November 1987, cited in *Utne Reader*, May/June 1989

[44] William Julius Wilson. When Work Disappears, *Political Science Quarterly*, Vol.111, Winter 1996-1997

[45] Leon H. Keyserling. The Problem of High Unemployment: Result of Muddled National Economic Policies, *Policy Studies Journal*, Vol. 8, Winter 1979 #3. p.349

[46] Ibid, p.351

Chapter 15: Solutions to the Problem of Mass Unemployment

[1] *Letter to the N.Y. Times*, 4/19/04, by Robert J. Reid, President, Center for Housing Policy.

2   John Miller: "The Surplus Vanishes" in *Dollars and Sense,* Nov. -Dec. 2001, p.26

3   Robert Higgs: "Billions More For Defense," *San Francisco Chronicle* Jan. 18, 2004. Higgs is a senior fellow in the Department of Political Economy at the Independent Institute in Oakland , California and author of the book: Crisis and Leviathan.

4   Ibid, p. 20.

5   Paul H. Nitze: "A Threat Mostly to Ourselves," *New York Times,* Oct. 28, 1999, p. A25

6   Seymour Melman: "Military State Capitalism," *The Nation,* May 20, 1991.

7   Ibid., p.?

8   Karen Talbot: "Peace Dividend: Critical Issues in the 1992 Elections," *Peoples Weekly World,* July 18, 1992.

9   Cited in Chalmers Johnson: *The Sorrows of Empire,* 2004

10   Cited in Donald Kaul: "Bush Policies Make Great Presidents Spin," *Progressive Populist,* Feb. 15, 2004

11   Ibid. p. 27

12   Ibid, p. 28

13   Rexford Tugwell: *In Search of Roosevelt,* p.265, 1972

14   Cited in Chalmers Johnson: *The Sorrows of Empire,* 2004

15   Ibid, p. 4

16   Ibid, p.5

17   John McDermott: "The Secret History of the Deficit," *The Nation,* April 21-28, 1962

18   Ibid, p. 146

19   Ibid, p. 146

20   *Wall St. Journal* April 6, 2004

21   "Dispatches": The Progressive Populist May 1, 2004

22   *Business Week* July 28, 2003

23   Paul Krugman, Dooh Nibor ["Robin Hood in reverse] Economics," *N.Y Times* June 1, 2004

24 This author is not an advocate of Buchanan's policies, but is in favor of giving him and all other political groups equal debate time in election campaigns.

25 Bruce Bliven, Max Lerner and George Soule: "The theory of Economic Expansion," New Republic, April 19, 1943. p. 537

26 Bliven, et al, p. 540

27 Congressional Record, Senate, May 27, 1943, p. 5037, cited in Marion Clausen: New Deal Planning, p. 231

28 Philip H. White: Termination of the NRPB, p.228

29 Robert M. Collins: The Business Response to Keynes 1929-1964, 1981, p. 57-58

30 See chapter 5

31 Note the Full Employment Act of 1946 was a toothless substitute for the 1945 Act but did stipulate the need for maximum employment opportunities.

32 Michael Harrington, "A Case for Democratic Planning," Irving Howe, ed., Alternatives: Proposals for America from the Democratic Left, 1984, Pantheon Books

33 For a very good account of the ideas of economic democrats see Kenneth M. Dolbeare's highly readable and excellent book: Democracy at Work: The Politics of Economic Renewal, 1984

34 See the chapter on Mergers and Acquisitions

35 For a very elaborate, detailed and thoughtful book on the how working people can run the economy, see Looking Forward, Participatory Economics for the Twenty First Century, by Michael Albert and Robin Hahnel, 1991, South End Press.